Best Wishes

Tony Tan

Best Wishes

Jerry Prior.

BRITAIN
IN OLD PHOTOGRAPHS

GREAT BRIDGE
REVISITED

TERRY PRICE

Sutton Publishing Limited
Phoenix Mill · Thrupp · Stroud
Gloucestershire · GL5 2BU

First published 2002

Reprinted 2002

Title page photograph: An early version of a car boot sale in Great Bridge Market Place, *c.* 1945, with a trader displaying his wares on the 'monkey bricks'. Pictured right is a West Bromwich Corporation No. 28 bus, which began operating a circular service between Great Bridge and Dartmouth Square, via Hill Top, on 6 April 1936. (*Ned Williams*)

British Library Cataloguing in Publication Data
A catalogue record for this book is available from the British Library.

ISBN 0-7509-2875-1

Typeset in 10.5/13.5 Photina.
Typesetting and origination by
Sutton Publishing Limited.
Printed and bound in England by
J.H. Haynes & Co. Ltd, Sparkford.

Dedicated to my wife, Beryl, who during the forty years of our marriage has unfailingly supported my involvement and historical interest in the local communities of Great Bridge and West Bromwich.

Royalties received by the author from this publication will be donated to the following churches:

Great Bridge Street Methodist Church
New Road Methodist Church
Ryders Green Methodist Church
Salem United Reform Church, Great Bridge
St Paul's Church, Golds Hill
St Peter's Church, Great Bridge

CONTENTS

A West Bromwich Corporation No. 76 short-working Daimler bus turns round in Great Bridge Market Place for the return journey to Birmingham, *c.* 1962. The premises of Joseph Wiltshire, pawnbroker and outfitters, stands out on the right, with hair stylist Adelaid Udall next door. (*David Wilson*)

Aerial view of the area around Great Bridge Street, *c.* 1962, showing, centre right, the eight locks section of Walsall Canal. At the top of the picture, between Ryder and Charles Streets, is William Street, while on the left, below Elwell and Richmond Streets, are the Wellington Tube Works. (*Geoff Pickering*)

INTRODUCTION

Great Bridge – the name conjures up visions of a magnificent long-forgotten bridge astride a vast river linking the two parishes of Tipton and West Bromwich. Visitors to Great Bridge, however, may be surprised to learn that although a river does indeed exist, there has never been a bridge of gigantic proportions in the locality. The prefix 'Great' in all probability was derived from the surrounding area, once known as 'Grete' or 'Greot', meaning gravel. Another theory is that as the words 'Greta' and 'Greet' were common Anglo-Saxon names for a river, the present-day name has evolved from an ancient reference to 'the bridge over the Greet'. There may have been a small bridge, possibly a wooden structure, or even just a ford as far back as Saxon times, when track routes from Dudley, Oldbury, Tipton, Wednesbury and West Bromwich are known to have converged at this river crossing. A bridge may also have been used by the Prior of Sandwell to gain access to his half acre of land and mill on the Tipton side of the river, which was given to the Benedictine order by the Lord of West Bromwich Manor around 1180. There was certainly a horse bridge in existence when Cromwell's troops crossed over it in 1646 on their way to lay siege to Dudley Castle, and local legend has it that the officer in command was so impressed with the structure's ability to support the movement of heavy cannon that he proclaimed it would be known henceforth as a 'great bridge'. Years later, following its reconstruction, a plaque is reputed to have been fixed to the bridge detailing the story but there is now no physical or documentary evidence to support the account. However, this small bridge is still in existence, to the rear of the Kwik-Save Supermarket car park in Fisher Street. Its authenticity as the site of an ancient bridge over the River Tame at Grete has, for many years, continued to be the subject of debate between local historians.

Great Bridge thus owes its very existence and development into an important trading and manufacturing area of the nineteenth and twentieth centuries to this modest but strategically important crossing over the River Tame. Indeed, many people new to the area unwittingly refer to Great Bridge as a 'town' when, of course, it has never achieved such a lofty status. There was a time, however, when this ambition could have become a reality. In the early nineteenth century, a group of houses between White Hall and Cop Hall formed three small streets named, respectively, Finch, Frances and Rogers. They were known as 'Paul's New Town', the name apparently derived from Sir Horace St Paul Bart of Ewart Park, Northumberland, owner of the land between Dunkirk and Great Bridge known as the Pump House Estate and also a large landowner in Tipton. The name 'Newtown' is still in use within the area although the street names have changed to Farley and Horton, the third having disappeared.

Early in the twentieth century Great Bridge could boast of having no less than three picture houses in the district. The first was situated within an Odd Fellows Hall in the

Market Place (1910), the second, the Victoria in Railway Street (1912), and the most well known, the Palace, on the corner of Slater Street, also first licensed in 1912.

It is not generally known, however, that a theatre was erected in Great Bridge prior to these. In 1884 Messrs Bates and Wakeman's Theatre of Varieties Company of Loughborough submitted plans to the Borough Surveyor's Office for the construction of a theatre in the West Bromwich part of Great Bridge on vacant land in Slater Street. These plans were subsequently approved by the West Bromwich Highway Committee on 8 April 1884. The theatre was a large prefabricated construction and of a 'portable' type, which after a few weeks or months, depending on the audiences, would have been dismantled before moving on to another venue, where the whole process was repeated.

Great Bridge North railway station, on the South Staffordshire Line, had the distinction of being Tipton's first when it opened on 1 May 1850, some two years before those at Dudley Port and Owen Street. This event underlined the importance of Great Bridge in the commercial activities of the Black Country during the nineteenth century.

Many people born in Great Bridge and the surrounding areas will be remembered for their outstanding achievements within the local community, but none more so than Alderman Reuben Farley, the first (and five times) Mayor of West Bromwich. Born at 146 Whitehall Road, Great Bridge on 27 January 1826, he was the greatest benefactor West Bromwich has ever known, and there are reminders of him everywhere. One is Farley Park, which was donated by him in 1891, mainly for the benefit of the people in the Greets Green and Great Bridge areas. Coincidentally, Joshua Churchman, who was also born in Whitehall Road, achieved a similar degree of fame when in 1966 he became the first Mayor of the new and enlarged County Borough of West Bromwich, which included both Tipton and Wednesbury. It was particularly fitting that the uniting of the two halves of Great Bridge under one authority as a result of this amalgamation should have taken place during his term of office.

Great Bridge has, of course, also had its share of unusual characters and one in particular came to mind while writing this introduction, Bertie Amos from William Street. Despite his advancing years he could be seen most days in the 1930s, '40s and '50s 'driving' the double-decker buses from his front seat position on the upper level. The love of his life, however, was the steamroller – whenever he saw one in Great Bridge he would follow it for miles. He spent so much time with the workmen that at the end of the week they gave him a 'wage packet' containing a few coppers, which pleased him enormously. Great Bridge in those days seemed alive with extrovert personalities – there was never a dull moment whether it was at school, at work, in a pub or just out shopping.

I hope, therefore, that this second selection of old photographs will again bring back many happy memories to all those who lived through what in retrospect were the 'golden years' of life in Great Bridge during the last century.

Terence J.H. Price
May 2002

Chapter One
Shops & Views

Shops in Great Bridge Market Place, 20 August 1986. Crumbs Confectioners acquired their premises from Robinsons around 1981, while next door Catering Hire's predecessor was, until 1985, Ella Fashions. John Bayliss traded in electrical goods, and later fishing tackle, from 1970 until closure in 1994 and prior to his ownership the shop was Stantons the tobacconist. Between 1975 and *c.* 1990 Central Carpets occupied the end property, which had previously been the Maypole Dairy Co., followed by Muriel's Wool Shop. (*Bob Binns*)

A pony and trap passes through the busy Market Place in Great Bridge, *c.* 1907. All the properties in this picture were built around 1865 and although there had been a market in front of the Limerick Inn since the early nineteenth century, the term 'market place' was not formally used as a postal or trade address until after 1870. (*Bev Pegg*)

Market day, pictured in June 1972, sixty-five years after the above photograph was taken from a similar position in New Road. The new premises of Lloyds Bank, centre background, between Whittall's Wines and the chemist, appear to be the only structural change that has occurred on this side of the Market Place in over 100 years. (*Jim Walters*)

A view across Great Bridge Market Place looking towards New Road, *c.* 1912. Samuel Saxon and Co., picture frame makers, are on the corner of Market Street (left) next to Joseph Wiltshire's furniture shop at 1 New Road. Raynes and Co., grocers, occupy the properties at 3 and 4 New Road which in 1918 were taken over by outfitters Arthur and Minnie Welch. (*Jim Houghton*)

Most of the properties shown in this picture of Great Bridge, *c.* 1960, date from around 1830 and are among the first to have been built in the area around the Market Place. The one exception is the premises occupied by W. Devis & Sons Ltd, built on the site of Thomas Collins' boot shop around 1912. (*Jim Walters*)

South Staffordshire tramcar No. 5, operating on the Dudley–Birmingham route, arrives in Great Bridge Market Place, *c.* 1912. The Limerick Inn stands between the approach roads to Horseley Heath left and New Road on the right. The pub's landlord, Thomas Brennand, was also the proprietor of three other licensed premises, all in West Bromwich: Cross Guns, New Hop Pole and the Malthouse Brewery in Bratt Street. (*Clive Murray*)

Great Bridge Market Place, *c.* 1940, showing the white road markings in use during the Second World War. The tram service on the No. 74 Birmingham–Dudley route had been replaced in 1939 by double-decker buses, one of which is just visible on the left. The Great Bridge Coffee House next to Beedles Ironmongers' store was at this time owned by Ellen M. Bedson, while the Limerick Inn's licensee was Arthur Cumberbatch. (*T.J.H. Price*)

New Road, Great Bridge, looking towards the Market Place, March 1981. Frank Cormell's New Era Wallpaper shop is at No. 7 (right) alongside what was once the entrance to Great Bridge South passenger railway station. (*Frank Wardle*)

The new frontage of Messrs, A.F. Welch, 2, 3 and 4 New Road, Great Bridge, *c.* 1939. This drapery business, established shortly after Arthur's marriage to Minnie Smith on 14 June 1908, was initially carried on from their home before being transferred in 1910 to a small warehouse in Whitehouse Street, Burnt Tree. By 1918 their commercial success had resulted in a move to the premises pictured right, where Arthur also continued to advance his interests in the Royal Liver Friendly Society, eventually becoming their District Manager. (*Beryl Jarvis*)

Market Street (formerly Limerick Passage), 6 August 1988. All of these buildings were later demolished to make way for a large traffic island and dual carriageway linking Great Bridge to the Black Country New Road. Mary's Sandwich Bar (left) was at one time the premises of Elizabeth Banner, music dealer. (*Jim Houghton*)

This view of Great Bridge Market Place, *c.* 1905, was originally published in an early *Wrench Series* of colour picture postcards which were occasionally overprinted with advertisements such as this one for Blackham's shop, pictured left. Thomas Blackham established his printing and stationery business here in 1883 having served his apprenticeship in the trade under Joseph Dawson of Burslem. In 1910 his son, Thomas William Blackham, inherited the firm which fifty-four years later was acquired by the printer Ian Smith. (*T.J.H. Price*)

New Road, Great Bridge, adjacent to W. Devis & Sons' abattoir and bacon factory. Right: an entrance to their lairages constructed alongside the old LMS Railway line. Centre: a rare sighting of St Luke's Mission Church, which stood here from 1901 until its demolition in 1967. (*Terry Scotland*)

The junction of Great Bridge Market Place and New Road, *c.* 1971, showing the transportation of a crane bogie, made by Thompson-Horseley Ltd, to Wellman Cranes of Darlaston by Wrekin Roadways. Following behind in the Triumph car is Thompson-Horseley's Transport Manager, Bill Wheale, the man in charge of these operations. (*Bill Wheale*)

One of Thomas Clayton's motor-driven tar boats about to pass under Brickhouse Lane Bridge on the Walsall Canal, having just negotiated the bottom lock of the eight locks flight, 2 June 1965. The railway bridge in the background carried the Great Bridge to Swan Village GWR line, which was closed to passenger traffic on 4 May 1964, and to freight in December 1967. (*David Wilson*)

The Toll End Communication Canal looking towards Brookhouse Bridge, 10 June 1969. The bridge carried Toll End Road past the perambulator company of Tan Sad Ltd, seen here on the left. This stretch of the canal opened in 1809 but by the end of 1966 it was no longer in use. (*Alan Price*)

Eleven years separate these two photographs of Horseley Bridge & Thomas Piggott's sports ground, previously owned by Triplex Foundry Ltd. The pictures were taken from the rear of 16 Clarkes Grove, Great Bridge, looking towards Ocker Hill and Wednesbury. The picture above shows a cricket match in progress around 1963 while below, on the same site in July 1974, houses are seen under construction. Note the absence of electricity pylons and Toll End MEB offices on the horizon in 1963. (*Jim Walters*)

A Midland Red bus passes the firm of Dale Dry Cleaners Ltd at 128 Horseley Heath in August 1962. These premises were taken over in 1971 by Geoffrey J. Lloyd, whose electrical, radio and television business, after thirty years' trading, is now the oldest of its kind in the Great Bridge area. Other shops in the picture, from left to right: Walter Reynolds, newsagents; the Nag's Head, public house; Albert and Harry Powell, cycle dealers; and Beryl's' ladies hairdresser. (*David Wilson*)

Leading the Great Bridge Trinity Methodist Church Sunday School anniversary parade, *c.* 1966, are the 7th Tipton Scouts (Great Bridge), seen here in New Road passing the premises of Walter Kendall, fruiterer and greengrocer. The Scouts have within their ranks, from left to right: Eric Shelley, Wilf Jones, Maurice Shelley, Terry Caswell, Tony Leach, Vic Grainger, Alan Roberts and Ben Dunn. (*Ron Greenfield*)

Horseley Heath, *c.* 1970, showing the Nag's Head pub (left), managed by Benjamin and Nellie Morgan. (It was renamed the Fusilier on 20 November 1998). One of the two tall houses pictured right (No. 121) was once occupied by George Hipkins, who later sold it to Alfred and Ethel Vanes. The other property (No. 122) was until 1969 the home of Arthur F. Welch and afterwards the offices of VEJAY insurance brokers, the forerunner of Penningtons. (*Alf Perks*)

People relaxing outside houses in Meeting Street, Horseley Heath, 19 August 1968. Further along on the right-hand corner is the Leopard Inn: it is clear from this rear vantage point that this was originally two separate buildings. Opposite, at 123–4 Horseley Heath, can be seen the premises of cycle dealers Albert and Harry Powell. (*Alan Price*)

Old houses in Ballfields, Great Bridge, July 1968, showing compulsory purchase notices on their frontages. This street, which links Horseley Heath with Tame Road, takes its name from an area surrounding the early nineteenth-century Golden Ball public house, which stood here until about 1930. (*Alan Price*)

Tame Road, Great Bridge, pictured in August 1968 with the Seven Stars pub and Salem Church in the distance, just beyond the parked cars. The road was known as Sheepwash Lane until around 1930 when, following reconstruction of the river bridge on the Tipton/West Bromwich border, it was renamed Tame Road. (*Alan Price*)

Horseley Heath looking towards Great Bridge, *c.* 1908, showing the post office (left), where Robert Crear was postmaster. According to an Ordnance Survey map of 1887 the whole of this turnpike road, from Dudley Port station to Swan Village, was once known as Great Bridge Street. By 1921, Hebron Hall would occupy the vacant space overlooked by a large 'Walkers Warrington Ale' sign. (*Clive Murray*)

Horseley Heath from the junction of Horseley Road, 9 August 1968. The centre of the picture shows Hebron Hall, which opened for worship in 1921. While most of the surrounding buildings have since been demolished, including the Prince Regent pub (behind the lorry), the hall continues to be used for religious services. (*Alan Price*)

Bagnall Street, Golds Hill, 18 January 1975, showing a WMTE Daimler Fleetline bus, on the No. 40 West Bromwich–Great Bridge circular route, approaching Eagle Lane railway crossings. Left of the bus is the scrap metal firm of John Cashmore Ltd, while on the right are constructional engineers Wilfred Robbins Ltd. Behind the Ratcliffs' sign is a dirt track road leading to an area known locally as 'the cracker'. (*David Wilson*)

The West Bromwich half of Great Bridge, *c.* 1942, looking towards Whitehall Road in the distance. Pork butcher George Hipkins' shop is extreme right with Freeman, Hardy and Willis footwear premises next door. The tramlines shown here, along with those in the Market Place, were taken up during the Second World War, leaving the remaining section in Great Bridge Street undisturbed until 1959. (*T.J.H. Price*)

Almost all these Great Bridge properties have changed ownership since this picture was taken in March 1981, the exceptions being Peplow & Thomas Insurance Services, Nos 75/77, and Hanson & Russell Ltd, Family Butcher at No. 59. Until its closure around 1934 the Golden Lion public house was also located along here, at No. 63, next door to greengrocers A.H. Adams & Sons Ltd. (*Frank Wardle*)

Great Bridge, pictured from the corner of Slater Street in March 1981. In the 1950s some of the biggest names in the retail trade opened premises at Great Bridge: F.W. Woolworth and Co. Ltd, Boots the Chemists and Tesco supermarket are all seen here on the left. Today these properties are occupied by Belmont Furnishing, Co-op Pharmacy and Shoprite. (*Frank Wardle*)

Residents of Horton Street, Great Bridge, with Beryl Heeley (left) and Doris Abbotts (right) sitting astride Stan Westwood's 350cc OHV Royal Enfield Model WD/CO motorcycle during the summer of 1953. In the background, from left to right: Stan Westwood, Emily Wherton, Jack Westwood, Arthur Heeley, Linda Abbotts. Horton Street contained one of the earliest housing developments in the Great Bridge area during the first part of the nineteenth century and under its former name of Frances Street was part of Sir Horace St Paul Bart's ambitious plan to build a 'new town' on his Pump House Estate. By 1849 Sir Horace was a large landowner in both Tipton and West Bromwich, with his holdings in the latter area alone amounting to 56 acres, including the Pump House Colliery. The street was also well known for having within it the Queen's Head public house, which along with their football team, was nicknamed 'Tommy Wright's' after its longest serving licensee. (*Doris Abbotts*)

The old tollhouse at the junction of Slater Street and Great Bridge, *c.* 1900. It was erected in the late eighteenth century but during its latter years, from 1899 to 1910, the property was occupied by tobacconist Edwin Steventon and finally hairdresser Frank Hedge, before being demolished to make way for the Palace Cinema, which opened in November 1912. (*T.J.H. Price*)

A West Bromwich Corporation No. 74 bus on the Dudley–Birmingham route approaches the Walsall Canal bridge in Great Bridge Street, 2 March 1963. Overlooking the canal locks was, until its closure in 1930, the Black Horse public house run by Rose and José Lopez Perez. In the background, next to Bannister & Thatcher chemists, the construction of a new shopping development is under way on the site of the Palace Cinema, which closed on 16 April 1960. (*David Wilson*)

'The big hill' in Richmond Street, July 1976, was until about 1949 an unadopted dirt road between Brickhouse Lane and the Elwell Street properties, pictured left. Three of Richmond Street's four houses were demolished in 1968, leaving only Ted and Queenie Nuttall's residence on the corner of Great Bridge Street still standing. (*T.J.H. Price*)

Floods in Great Bridge Street at the junction with Charles Street, *c.* 1937. The large white house was occupied by two separate families, Wallace and Mary Jane Hill at 203a, with Ethel and Percy Sargent at 203. Previous residents had been James Bayley in 1927 and Albert Aston, painter and decorator, in 1892. Beyond the telephone box, at No. 201 was Alice and Frederick Round's house, behind which Thomas Moss established a brass foundry around 1870. (*T.J.H. Price*)

Joe Shelley (left) and colleagues re-laying granite setts (monkey bricks) between the tramlines in Great Bridge Street, *c.* 1935. These tracks were taken up in 1959, twenty years after the tram service had ceased on 1 April 1939. Rebecca and Thomas Ore's greengrocery shop can be seen on the right, while opposite is the Turk's Head public house. (*Dorothy Wheatley*)

Land adjoining Great Bridge Street and Victoria Street, Swan Village, acquired for extensions by the Phoenix Steel Tube Co., *c.* 1929. It was previously the site of Messrs. J. and S. Roberts iron foundry, after whom the nearby canal bridge was named. By coincidence the photographer has captured a remarkable view of the Swan Village gas tank under its final phase of construction. (*David Airey*)

Billy Hyde's greengrocery and tobacconist shops at 248–54 Great Bridge Street, *c.* 1930. The greengrocery business (left), was established around 1868 by Billy's grandparents Mary and Jeremiah Sheldon. Daughter Mary Ann and son-in-law Richard Hyde took over the property in 1896, converting the other half into a tobacconist shop in 1920. Their son Billy, however, was the person who effectively ran the business until its closure in 1963. (*Ernest Hyde*)

Atlas Grove, Greets Green, 1938. It was named after the nearby Atlas Ironworks of Edward Parkes & Co. Between 1937, when the first house was occupied, and *c.* 1952 the road surface remained unadopted in the condition seen here. It also provided traffic access to the Steel Equipment Company Ltd,which, despite protestations from local residents, continued until the firm's closure in May 1982. (*South Staffs Water*)

Floods in Oldbury Road at the junction with Union Road, Greets Green, *c.* 1960. The building on the left, where Mrs Gwynne and her daughter Mary are looking out of the window, was from 1886 until about 1930 the Vulcan Inn. Pumps were borrowed from the Civil Defence to extract water from the cellars of houses opposite, two of which show Florence Carter and her son on their doorsteps. (*Jill Spooner*)

The top of the eight locks flight on the Walsall Canal showing Alan 'Caggy' Stevens operating a narrow boat assisted by his horse Jean, 8 July 1965. In the background can be seen Ryders Green Road bridge with the Eight Locks public house nearby. (*David Wilson*)

Whitehall Road, Great Bridge, 14 April 1970, with Conex-Sanbra Ltd dominating the background. Conex Works was established in 1929 under the name Patent Copper Couplings Co. but by 1933 they had been acquired by the Sanbra Engineering Company. Conex-Terna, a wholly owned subsidiary of Sanbra, was formed in 1937, taking over the assets of the Patent Copper Couplings Co. In 1962 the name changed to Conex-Sanbra and after merging with IBP Group in 1994 they became known as IBP Conex. (*Alan Price*)

Pictured in front of Joseph Stevens' bakery and confectionery shop at 192 Oldbury Road, Greets Green, are his wife Ellen and baby son Derrick, *c.* 1935. The premises were acquired around 1928 from Alfred Hughes, who had previously run a general store from here. Within twelve months of his purchase, however, Joseph, whose parents had a bakers' shop in Bull Street, West Bromwich, also began making bread on the premises, delivering to customers by horse and cart. So successful was the business that by the early 1930s Joseph and his wife were in a position to buy not only their own property but also the house next door, which they subsequently rented out. These buildings were known as Vulcan Terrace, possibly named after the adjoining Vulcan public house (No. 194). Indeed, many other properties in the area also included 'Vulcan' in their title, such as the nearby Vulcan Iron Foundry and the Vulcan Tube Works. Around 1968 Vulcan Terrace became subject to a compulsory purchase order and, sadly, the shop and bakery were closed down. Joe and Nell, as they were known locally, retired to a bungalow in Wombourne, thus ending a family tradition of bakers spanning four generations. (*Jill Spooner*)

Benjamin Bird Allsopp and his grandson George Allsopp pose in front of their newsagents shop at 198 Greets Green Road, *c.* 1937. The business was established in 1904 by Benjamin and his wife Hannah Maria, who had taken over the property from Henry Law. Prior to this, however, Benjamin had been a mill furnaceman at Edward Parkes and Co., sheet iron manufacturers at Albion. The shop, pictured here decorated for King George VI's coronation in 1937, has above the doorway a demolition order which led to the building of new offices on the site shortly afterwards. These were eventually superseded by warehouse units, which form part of the present-day Queens Court Industrial Estate. In the meantime replacement premises for the old shop were obtained a few doors away at No. 206, which carried on under Benjamin's name until 1946. The business then passed to his granddaughter Clara Randall who, together with her husband Arthur, continued to trade until 1968, when her cousin George Allsopp took over. It was sold to Tony Rudge *c.* 1988. The property, now known as Carol's News, changed hands again in January 2001 when it was acquired by Muserat Khan. (*Ben Whale*)

Frederick J. Pearson stands in the doorway of his electrical and wireless shop at 73 Great Bridge, *c.* 1932. Fred had been a self-employed electrician before becoming the first occupant of these newly built premises around 1930. Both his and the next door property at No. 71 were, in fact, extension frontages added to very old private houses set back some distance from the main road. However, his ownership of the business did not last very long because by 1934 the shop had been taken over by James Gripton, who was also the proprietor of similar outlets in High Street and Paradise Street at West Bromwich. The Great Bridge premises continued to operate as an electrical, radio and later television business under a number of different owners throughout the 1930s, '40s and '50s until it was eventually converted into a menswear shop run by Frederick and Edna Groom. By this time, however, both Nos 73 and 71 had been combined into one shop, as No. 73. Amazingly, the original 1930 window of Frederick Pearson's shop has survived intact and now forms part of the frontage to estate agent Paul Dubberley & Co. (*Colin Boyes*)

Alfred Kirkham's off-licence and general stores at 34B William Street, Great Bridge, *c.* 1928. Since it began trading in the 1870s the business has had a number of proprietors, the first being Gifford Wheate. He was followed by John Tilley in 1892, John Holden in 1898 and Alfred Asbury in 1906. In 1915 Joseph Harrison began a three-year occupancy which preceded Alfred Kirkham's acquisition in 1918. Although the business traded under his name for the next thirty-eight years, it was his wife Laura who effectively ran the shop while Alfred was in the employ of Marsh & Baxters in Dale End, Birmingham. During the 1920s there were also five other businesses in William Street: at No. 14 William Harrison's fish and chip shop; No. 46 William Yeomans coal dealer; No. 49 Abel Crump's general store (later Oliver Bossward); No. 60 Sarah Holyhead's general store; and at No. 89 the Plough & Harrow public house. Alfred Kirkham died in 1955, and following his wife Laura's death in 1956 the shop closed. The property was later demolished as were the rest of the houses in William Street, the land around Kirkham's shop being subsequently purchased by R. Cruickshank Ltd of Charles Street. From left to right: Laura Turner, Phyllis Turner and Laura Kirkham. (*Phyllis Shadwell*)

Charlie's café, corner of Whitehall Road and Great Bridge, *c.* 1986. Prior to Ethel and Retlaw (Charlie) Talbot taking over in 1949 the premises had been a butcher's shop successively owned by Charles, Samuel and Thomas Breatt (*c.* 1900), Reuben Scragg (*c.* 1938) and during the 1940s a family named Field. In 1976 the café was sold to Brenda Cashmore who continued the business under Charlie's name until closure in 1988. The café and houses, including the home of photographer James Price pictured right, were demolished in 1989 prior to ironfounders James W. Shenton Ltd acquiring the land. (*Susan Stokes*)

Bronze-breasted turkeys hang from the ceiling in this Christmas 1950 interior view of family butcher George Hipkins' premises, Great Bridge. The staff pictured here are, from left to right: -?-, Dennis Edwards, Harold ?, ? Baker, Iris Thomas, Phylis Durden, -?-.
(*Stanley Durden*)

The 1950 Christmas window display of family butcher George Hipkins at 60–64 Great Bridge. These premises were originally three separate properties before George's acquisition in 1912. Following the death of George Hipkins in 1938, control of the business passed to his son Gilbert, who around 1955 sold it to George Samworth Snr. The firm continued under his and George Junior's ownership for another twenty-five years before finally closing in 1980. (*Stanley Durden*)

Whitehall Road, Great Bridge, with Tinsley Street on the left, May 1971. The air raid shelter near the sign of James W. Shenton was the headquarters of an ARP unit during the Second World War. The passage to the right of Rose and William Homer's florist shop approached houses once known as York Buildings, with Whitehall Lodge nearby, the one-time home and medical practice of Dr Douglas Martin Spring. (*Alf Perks*)

This evocative picture of Great Bridge market trader Betty Aston, a resident of Brickhouse Lane, was taken in 1969 on the triangular forecourt of the Limerick Inn where she and her sister Lily Haynes sold general household goods between 1948 and 1970. Although a market had been held on this spot since the early part of the nineteenth century the site had always belonged to the successive owners of the Limerick Inn. In the early 1970s Mitchells & Butlers decided to use the land as a car park for their public house, and as a consequence the market agreement which had existed between the brewery and generations of the Wordsworth family was cancelled. Shortly after this decision the market was transferred to the corner of nearby Mill Street, but that site was also closed down not long afterwards owing to a lack of support from local shoppers. A new indoor market was eventually established by Ted Skett on the West Bromwich side of Great Bridge which was opened by comedian Larry Grayson in October 1979. (*Birmingham Post & Mail/Derek Aston*)

Shop staff pictured behind the cooked meats counter inside the premises of George Hipkins, family butcher, *c.* 1957. From left to right: Walter Clarke, Larry Turner, Arthur Jones, Trevor Dunn, Mary Barnes, Jack ?, Mary Woodhall, Joe Bates. (*Ray Barnfield*)

The Central Pharmacy, 23 Market Place, Great Bridge,
c. 1910. These premises, owned by Matthew Henry
Griffith between 1906 and 1922, had been a chemist's
shop since the building was erected in 1865. Probably
the best known and certainly the longest occupant was
Simon Winroope, who from 1922 dispensed medicines
here for over forty years. The series of attractive brick
arches forming the shop's frontage was also a feature of
the Lloyds Bank building next door at No. 22 and is
reminiscent of a similar style adopted by the stationers
Mark and Moody of Stourbridge. The Black Country had
always attracted vendors of patent medicines and herbal
remedies, and some pharmacies managed to keep these
practices alive while pioneering the development of the
modern drug industry. These traditions were graphically
portrayed in 1910 when an advertisement appeared in
the local press showing the Central Pharmacy in Great
Bridge offering the following remedial specialities: 'Snow
Cream for Rough and Chapped Hands 6d and 9½d per
bottle', 'Face-ache Mixture, 1s per bottle', and 'Butlers
Parasitic Hair Wash, an effective Children's Hair Lotion,
6d per bottle'. (*Ned Williams*)

Absalom Withnall stands in the doorway of his hatters'
shop at 6 New Road, Great Bridge, c. 1910. The property
had only three previous occupants, all of them hatters,
William Atkins becoming the first around 1870. He was
followed by Charles Slade in 1880 and William Palmer in
1888. Ten years later, in 1898, Absalom Withnall
became the proprietor and traded here for the next
thirty-nine years, until in 1937 the property was
purchased and converted to a corn and seed merchant's
business by Albert H. Hodson. It is not known who was
responsible for the enormous eye-catching top hat seen
over the door but in the nineteenth and twentieth
centuries it was quite common for signs such as these to
be erected outside shop premises. Another example was
displayed opposite, at 117 New Road, where boot and
shoe manufacturer Benjamin Sowry had a large clog
hanging above the frontage of his shop. The building
pictured here survived until the 1990s when it was
demolished to make way for a traffic island which formed
part of the Great Bridge link to the Black Country New
Road. (*T.J.H. Price*)

William and Lucy Bagnall's 'high class' ladies and children's outfitters' shop at 119–20 Horseley Heath was in reality the continuation of a business established during the late nineteenth century by Lucy's father Francis Reynolds. It was he who opened their original Jubilee Buildings shop in 1888 at 135 Horseley Heath, where he described himself as a wardrobe and general dealer. Of all the businesses in Great Bridge probably none was more prolific than Bagnalls when it came to advertising and creating slogans, the most famous of course being 'The Talk Of The Town'. The delightful publicity card pictured here dates from March 1943 and is an example of those given as a keepsake to all customers entering their premises. (*Eileen Whitehouse*)

Lucy and William Bagnall stand outside their recently acquired clothiers' shop at 135 Horseley Heath, 1912. The business, established in 1888, had been passed on to them by Lucy's mother, Elizabeth Reynolds, but they were not to remain here very long because within a year they had transferred to new premises at 119–20 Horseley Heath. During the 1920s and 1930s the Bagnall family also involved themselves in the local community to such an extent that outings to the countryside were often organised for their customers. The largest of these outings was reported in the *Tipton Herald* of 15 July 1933 which stated that 'this colossal contingent of over 400 people from Great Bridge were accommodated in thirteen Midland Red buses'. For many years Lucy also represented the Horseley Heath Ward on Tipton Council and from 1941 to 1943 was Deputy Mayor to Arthur Edwin Bolton. In 1946 their son Edwin entered the firm, which at this time employed a total of twelve female staff. Indeed, the shop was so busy that it remained open each day from 8 a.m. to 8 p.m. Sadly, the business, which according to its slogan was once 'The Talk Of The Town', closed down during the 1970s. (*Eileen Whitehouse*)

Albert Edward Bourne, house furnisher, 134 Horseley Heath, *c.* 1953. Albert's ambition to own his own business goes back to the early 1930s when he became an agent for the National Clothing & Supply Co. of Wolverhampton. This entailed canvassing for potential customers, which he did from his home at 62 Tame Road, Great Bridge, building up a large credit round in the process. At the start of the Second World War he introduced fancy goods and toys into his round when these were very hard to obtain, all paid for on credit or by people running clubs. In 1946 he purchased John Backhouse's hardware business at 112 Horseley Heath which was quickly expanded to include fancy goods. A second shop was opened in 1952 at 134 Horseley Heath providing a much larger trading area which could accommodate furniture, nursery goods, carpets and linens. This property had previously been Mackindoe's sewing factory and before that the Grinders Arms public house. After Albert's retirement in 1965 the business was sold to L.D. Gupta, who appointed Ron Welch, the present owner of Decoron Wallpapers Ltd of West Bromwich, as Manager. From left to right: Fanny Martin, Gillian Waters, Gwen Waters, Win Bourne, Edith Bourne, -?-, Albert Bourne. (*Gwen Waters*)

The nation's obsession with its favourite pastime of queuing during the austere years following the Second World War, is exemplified in this picture taken outside Reynolds' hairdressing and newsagent's shop 33 Market Place, Great Bridge, on 2 November 1948. The crowds, which extend beyond the Nags Head pub and Mill Street in the background, are, surprisingly, queuing for fireworks! At the end of the war and on Guy Fawkes' night, government restrictions on the supply of fireworks had meant that people could not celebrate in the traditional manner. William Reynolds, seen here at the head of the queue, was a friend of Mr Wilder, owner of the Wilders Fireworks Company and as a consequence he obtained stocks before anyone else in Great Bridge. However, in order to ensure a fair distribution, his customers were confined to purchasing just one mixed bag of fireworks, costing in those days the princely sum of 2*s* 6*d*. Among the crowd, between the two ladies wearing spectacles at the front, is Brickhouse Lane resident Mary Martin. (*Walter Reynolds*)

Ernest Victor Jukes stands on the doorstep of his grocers' shop at the corner of Scott Street and Horseley Heath, *c.* 1965. It was around 1924 that he took over these premises from his father Victor, who in 1910 had purchased the business as a going concern from William H. Smith. These corner shops were once part of the late Victorian urban spread of tightly packed rectangular streets and have tended to disappear with the demolition and clearance of such areas: this property suffered the same fate in the early 1970s. Contrary to popular belief, however, they have not all become extinct, although many can now be regarded as an 'endangered species'. (*Eric Hodgetts*)

Stan Buckle's gentlemen's hairdressing saloon at 212A Horseley Heath, *c.* 1967. The gents' hairdresser of today has to keep up with the times and display a sense of fashion and style. Gone are the days of premises displaying striped poles with barbers who only knew one type of haircut, 'short-back-and-sides'. Not many modern hairdressing businesses, however, can claim the same longevity as the one pictured here which has, since the nineteenth century, continued to operate from the same address. It was established in 1899 by Joseph Baker who had previously been a hairdresser and newsagent at 3 Market Place, Great Bridge (opposite Wiltshire's). The business continued for the next forty years with Joe at the helm until in 1939 it was taken over by Stan Buckle. These hairdressing premises remained in Stan's hands for over thirty years before being acquired by Alan Doggett on 16 January 1972. The old building was replaced in 1973 by a new, modern hairdressing salon and shop which is still going strong under Alan Doggett's successful ownership. (*Alan Doggett*)

Chapter Two
Pubs & Events

The Three Crowns, 10 Great Bridge Street, Swan Village, December 1965. Dating from
c. 1865, when it was run by Thomas Glover, the pub survived for just over 100 years before
finally closing in 1969. During the last seven years of operation it was managed by Arthur
and Iris Williams. A private house now occupies the site. (*Edwin Yates*)

The Limerick Inn, Market Place, *c.* 1950. At this time the landlord was Philip Daw. When Joseph Bagnall took over in 1880 he changed the pub's name to the Wrexham, but following Thomas Brennand's acquisition of the property in 1894 it was promptly changed back to the Limerick Inn, which it has been ever since. (*Robin Pearson*)

'Lucas's Lion Inn regulars, Sunday morning breakfast trip from Great Bridge to Stourport in June 1953. In the doorway are licensees Ted and Alice England. Back row, left to right: -?-, Walter Salt, -?-, Sam Wall, Dick Nicholls, Sam Wall Jnr. Middle section: Les Packwood, Harry Cartwright, Jack Homer, 'Snowy' Lappage, Gordon Baker, Jack Gwynn, Harry Gilbert, Richard Hill, Jack Randle, Freddy Gilbert, Bill Stanley. Front row: Freddy Smith, -?-, Wilf Bamford, -?-, Harry Hobson, -?-, Walter Stone, -?-. (*Ronnie James*)

Violet Bourne's Orange Tree Stores off-licence at 141 Horseley Heath, August 1968. The business was established in 1890 by George Cornwell, a general dealer, who sold it to Abraham Lockhart in 1905. Some time around 1920 the store also became an off-licence and remained so until its closure on 2 November 1969. (*Alan Price*)

The upstairs lounge of the Prince Regent, Horseley Heath, during a darts team social evening, *c.* 1970. Among the outer row, left to right: Bill Billingham, Eddie Chilton, Doreen Steen, Florence Cash, Don Chilton, Margaret Vickerstaff, Wilf Vickerstaff (licensee), Fred Weaver, Gordon Shaw, Linda Hodgkiss, Sam Potts, Bill Potts. Centre section: Tony Parker, Robert Cooksey, Henry Delicott, Peggy Delicott, Cliff Short, Ron Short, Harry Hollowood, Ron Edwards, Terry Moore, Joyce Moore, Ted Sheldon, Margaret Moore. (*Margaret Phillips*)

The Star Hotel, 176 Horseley Heath June 1969, where Leslie Tansley was the licensee. Records show that in 1860 the first landlord was local hinge-maker William Doughty, the father of Councillor William Wooley Doughty JP. One hundred and thirty-one years later, on 15 July 1991, while under the management of Robert Pinner, the name was changed to the Port N'Ale. (*Alan Price*)

Customers of the White Rose public house, Horseley Heath, on an outing to the Cotswolds organised by licensees James and Maud Durkin, *c.* 1952. Among the back row, from left to right: Henry Taylor, Eric Gibson, Billy Taylor. Middle section: Bessie Bayley, ? Gibson, Rachel Bayley, Rosie Ford, George Buswell, ? Mumford. Front row: Mary Ford, Christine Durden, Arthur Ford, -?-, Joe Bayley, ? Mumford, Daisy Taylor, Matty ?. (*Ken Bayley*)

The Shakespeare Inn, 25 Bridge Road, Toll End, 8 September 1968, with Albert Dunkley as the licensee. The name 'Shakespeare' was probably chosen by its first licensee, John Hathaway who around 1870 also ran a pawnbroker's business from here. One can only imagine the detrimental effect that this combination of interests had on some of his customers' lives. After having only six licensees in a 100-year period the pub closed on 27 July 1969. (*Alan Price*)

An interior view of the Shakespeare Inn, Bridge Road, Toll End, showing a harvest festival display, *c.* 1946. Gladys Walker, wife of the licensee Charlie Walker, can also be seen behind the bar. (*Dorothy Cartwright*)

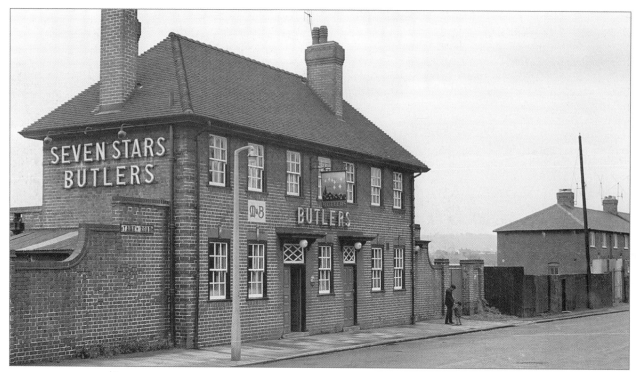

A view of the Seven Stars, 45 Tame Road, Great Bridge, in August 1968 when Edwin and Florence Turner were the licensees. This 1920s building replaced a much older structure dating from around 1860 when landlord John Lloyd lived there. Until about 1930 the whole of the highway in front of the pub was known as Sheepwash Lane. (*Alan Price*)

Friends and neighbours gather in the Shakespeare Inn, Bridge Road, Toll End, for the harvest festival celebrations of about 1946. Among the customers are: Tom Powell, Jack Powell, Fred Powell, William Powell, Eliza Powell, Olive Powell, Frank Bradley, Jack Cartwright, Harold Shaw, Fred Guest, Sam Hirons, Joe Davies, Joe Dolman, Charlie Dolman, Dan Sherwood, Albert Price, Olive Hodgkinson, William Barnfield, Jack Rushton, Jack Darby. (*Dorothy Cartwright*)

The Dewdrop Inn, 33 Toll End Road, *c.* 1932. The name over the door is that of Joseph Richards, landlord from 1930 until 1940. There had been only five previous holders of the licence stretching back to 1855, when Joseph Gwilt was recorded as being the first. The others were Joseph Thomas 1880–8, Ann Thomas 1888–1902, Albert Dunkley 1902–26, Alfred Hodgetts 1926–30. (*Valerie Walker*)

Pictured in front of the Hop & Barleycorn Inn, Toll End Road, *c.* 1902, are licensees Ann and Henry Morris, whose son Freddy was to gain future fame with West Bromwich Albion FC. The building, demolished in about 1905, stood on a site later occupied by the Tan Sad Perambulator Company. (*Jean Weston*)

The Tipton Tavern, 57 New Road, Great Bridge, June 1969, when George Summers was the licensee. During an enemy bombing raid of 17 May 1941, the previous pub on the site, dating from the early 1820s, was completely destroyed. Roger Preece, landlord since 1914, fortunately survived after being buried by debris while sheltering in the cellar. On 13 September 1996 this historic pub's name was changed to the Hallbridge Arms. (*Alan Price*)

Dennis Day was 'Mine Host' when this picture of the King's Arms, Toll End Road, was taken on 2 August 1968. The pub's licence dates from before 1845 when an entry in *Kelly's Directory* shows Chenaniah Taylor as the licensee. This hostelry has since been replaced by a new and luxurious building which opened under the management of Trigfor Morrell on 16 November 1987. (*Alan Price*)

The Railway Inn, 92 New Road, Great Bridge, better known as 'The Fourpenny Shop', June 1969. On the right of the building can be seen a passage leading to Great Bridge North railway station which, like the original Railway Inn on this site, opened in 1850. Gary Burke was the licensee at the time of this picture. (*Alan Price*)

The Griffin Inn, 90 New Road, Great Bridge, pictured in June 1969 during the management of Frank Regan. Originally owned by Showells Brewery of Langley and changing to Ansells on 30 May 1960, the pub had no less than twenty-one licensees during its final eighteen years of life. The premises, first licensed around 1860, closed on 5 May 1978 and were afterwards sold, along with other adjacent properties, to A.H. Adams & Sons Ltd. (*Alan Price*)

Opposite the Methodist chapel in Harvills Hawthorn stood the rather grandly named Royal Exchange Hotel, pictured here around 1934 when it was kept by Frederick Hassell. The pub dates from around 1870, James Tipler being recorded as the first licensee. At this time it sold only 'home brew' but afterwards was taken over by William Butler & Co., who in 1960 were subsumed by Mitchells & Butlers. For almost a hundred years it had remained just a beer house until 4 April 1962, when a spirits licence was obtained by the then landlord Albert Lawrence. Fifteen years later on 8 September 1977 the premises closed with Gordon Stevens on record as the last licensee. Standing on the doorstep from left to right are: Frank Hassell, ? Hassell. (*T.J.H. Price*)

'Joe Butler's' Spring Cottage, 155 Harvills Hawthorn, 1954, on the occasion of Joe's retirement after thirty years as landlord. Dating from around 1858 when Richard Butler was licensee, the pub eventually closed on 4 October 1961. Among the back row: ? Highfield, Harold Whitehouse, Ray Homer, Arthur Cope, Mary Read, Elsie Pickerill. Middle section: Arthur Cope Snr, Billy Walker, Joe Butler Jnr, Arthur Reed. Front row: Joseph Butler, Elizabeth Butler, Joan Butler, Marjorie Butler. (*Lily Phillips*)

The present appearance of the Miners Arms at 58 Bagnall Street, Golds Hill, has changed somewhat since this picture was taken in April 1965, when Ernest George Miller was licensee. Today it is the sole survivor of an era when there were over twenty pubs in the immediate vicinity of Golds Hill. (*T.J.H. Price*)

King George VI's coronation celebrations in May 1937 outside 'Merthers' Britannia Inn, Pikehelve Street, Golds Hill. Back row, left to right: Tom Harper, Jacob Beddows, Alf Coole, Elizabeth Coole, Arthur Price, Harry Cowles, Florence Simcox, Amy Coole, -?-, Martha Merther, William Merther (licensee), Jack Bayliss, Cyril Harper, Ada Beddows, Sam Jones, Tom Norton, Jack Hughes. Front row: Ruth Harper, Elizabeth Foster, Violet Price, Mary Loveland, William Hughes, Annie Cowles, Elsie Taylor, Lucy Hughes, Alf Foster. (*Elsie Mills*)

A Christmas party for Wellington Tube Works employees' children held in 1953 at the old social club situated in what was formerly known as Blades Street. Eight years after the event pictured here the club was transferred to new premises alongside their main offices in Brickhouse Lane. Interestingly, during the 1930s the whole of Blades Street, which linked Brickhouse Lane with Great Bridge Street, was closed to the public having been totally consumed by the Tube Works. Fourth row, left to right: -?-, Maureen Jinks, Sheila Hill, Margaret Knowles, -?-. Third row: -?-, Keith Markham, Ann Markham, -?-, Victor Markham. Second row: Brenda Markham, Susan Markham, -?-, -?-, -?-, -?-. (*Brenda Stokes*)

A fund-raising concert organised by the Mayor of West Bromwich, Councillor Joshua Churchman JP, at the Wellington Tube Works Social Club, Brickhouse Lane, Great Bridge, 10 February 1967, in aid of the Lord Mayor of Birmingham's appeal for the mentally handicapped (West Bromwich Branch). Among those in the picture, from left to right: Ted Sheldon, Bill Woodward, George Spooner, Fred Phillips, Joshua Churchman (Mayor), Horace Hirons, Louie Hirons, Frank Northall. Centre: Edith and Tom Corbett, Violet Churchman (Mayoress), Albert Diggett. (*Joshua Churchman*)

The Plough & Harrow public house pictured here in 1938 was, along with many of the other buildings in William Street, erected around 1855 when plots of land in this area of Great Bridge were being advertised for sale by the Victoria Permanent Building Society. William Street itself was described at the time as 'newly laid out' according to the *Midland Counties Herald*. The original status of this pub, however, was probably that of a private house but by 1870 it had become a home-brew beer house under the ownership of John George, its first licensee. John Copper (1890–1906) and James Hunt followed until 1910 when Tom and Elizabeth Withington took it over, establishing themselves over the next thirty-four years as the pub's longest serving licensees. Another notable and long-serving landlord was John Whittingham who, together with his wife Hilda, occupied the premises from 1944 to 1967. During the hundred years of its operation, from John George to George Eaton, the pub had a total of only eight licensees. (*Keith Hodgkins*)

The Rose & Crown, 108 Brickhouse Lane, Great Bridge, *c.* 1930. George Sheldon was landlord here for an amazing fifty-one years (1887 to 1938) before being succeeded by Frank Corbett, who then held the licence until 1950. The pub finally closed in 1956, almost 100 years after Daniel Lawrence first opened it around 1860. (*Robin Pearson*)

The (top) Beehive, 112 Brickhouse Lane, Great Bridge, August 1968, with Robert Batchelor as licensee. It was opened in 1885 by licensee Elijah Parsons, who continued until 1910 before handing over to the appropriately named Moses Dunn. The pub is still thriving, although Brickhouse Lane is now closed to vehicular through-traffic at this point. (*Alan Price*)

The bar of the Wellington Inn, Great Bridge Street during their domino team's celebration supper, *c.* 1956. Back row, left to right: Jim Latham, Bill Jones, Cliff Markham, -?-, Tom Burns, Jacky Burns, Luke Dunne, Joe Markham, Ike Dunne, Horace Markham, -?-, -?-, Stan Powell, -?-. Seated clockwise around the table bottom left: Jim Powell, -?-, ? Rochelle, Arthur Cartwright, Jim Green, Ben Hill, -?-, -?-, Colin Boyes, John Parry, Len Ball, Freddy Glover, Fred Markham, James Senior (licensee), -?-. Top centre: Elizabeth Senior. (*Doris Smith*)

The (bottom) Beehive, 246 Great Bridge Street, 19 July 1969, when Leonard Keegan was the licensee. Dating from the 1850s this public house had only four licensees during the first 100 years of its life, Thomas Davis (1852–98), Charles Ingram (1898–1906), Emily Ingram (1906–10) and George 'Monkey' Jackson (1910–52). In contrast, another seventeen would follow before Pargon Singh Cheema became the last landlord prior to the pub's closure on 22 August 1988. (*Andrew Maxam*)

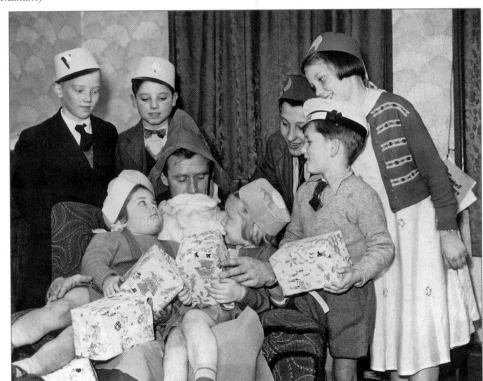

Santa Claus, alias Vic Buckingham, Manager of West Bromwich Albion FC, visits the King's Arms public house, 106 Great Bridge Street, Christmas 1954. Licensees Cliff and Ida Edwards had organised a party for customers' children, some of whom are pictured here with 'Santa'. Back row, left to right: Graham Glover, Derek Harris, Maurice Knight, Maureen Jinks. Front row: Denise Edwards, Vic Buckingham, -?-, Peter Edwards. (*Ida Edwards*)

Celebrating at the Wellington Inn, Great Bridge Street, *c.* 1955, are members and guests of their cup-winning domino team. Back row, left to right (standing): -?-, Joe Markham, Ernie Markham, Jack Powell, Stan Powell. Second row, left table: Len Ball, Ray Markham, Arthur Cartwright, Fred Markham, Joe Green, Jim Latham, Jim Powell. Front row: Isiah Powell, Colin Boyes, John Parry, Luke Dunne, Ted Smith, -?-, -?-, Dennis ?, Tom Lloyd. Right table: Cliff Markham, -?-, Ike Dunne, Dennis Beasley, Bernard Morris, Gerald Jackson, Sam Knowles. (*Vera Morris*)

Christmas 1953 at the King's Arms, 106 Great Bridge Street, where licensees Cliff and Ida Edwards are hosting a party for customers' children. Back row, left to right: -?-, Ida Edwards, Jessie Jinks, Ria Knight, -?-, Ruby Fletcher, -?-, Emily Harris. Left side table: Maureen Jinks, Graham Glover, Martin Harris. Right side table: Reg Gould, Derek Harris. Front: Raymond Jinks, Maurice Knight, Eddie Hill, Jean Powell. (*Ida Edwards*)

The Golden Cup, 42 Great Bridge Street, photographed on 26 May 1965 when Joseph Grice was landlord. The first licence for these premises was obtained around 1865 by Thomas Rusby, who held it for the next thirty years, prior to Thomas Neale's acquisition in 1895. The pub closed 5 March 1978 and was thereafter converted to alternative business use. (*Andrew Maxam*)

Licensee Joseph Grice and his wife Gladys in 1964 behind the bar of the Golden Cup in Great Bridge Street which they ran from April 1959 until July 1969. The pub, which was successively owned by William Butler & Co., Mitchells & Butlers and finally Bass, had another four licensees before Gordon Richards became the last on 6 January 1977. (*Barry Grice*)

The Swan Inn, Swan Village, *c.* 1958. This hostelry was built in 1860 to replace a much older Swan Inn erected on the site in 1550. During the eighteenth and nineteenth centuries it was also the venue for court proceedings and at one time contained a library. Richard Sterry was the licensee in 1638 but more recent occupants have been Samuel and Ann Butler (1948–68), Joyce Partridge (1968–85), and Sukhbir Singh from 1985 until its closure in 1992. (*T.J.H. Price*)

The Swan Inn darts team, Swan Village pictured in October 1954 celebrating at their annual dinner after a successful season in the Greets Green League. Knock-Out Cup winners and league runners-up, they also won the British Legion Cup and the coveted West Bromwich Darts Federation's T. Dugdale Cup. (*Joyce Partridge*)

The Bird In Hand, 9 Phoenix Street, Swan Village, *c.* 1982, when Ronald Booker was the licensee. At the time of its opening in 1875 the landlord's name was, rather appropriately, Joseph Tipler. Another early licensee between 1914 and 1922 was William 'Caggy' Roberts, who afterwards moved to the White Swan in Vernon Street, Greets Green. The pub closed on 26 May 1999 and is now Antonio's Dial-A-Pizza. (*T.J.H. Price*)

The George, 109 Phoenix Street, Swan Village, *c.* 1982, when Jeffrey Whitehouse was the resident landlord. Noted licensees from the past include Sylvia Gould 1914–22, Frank and Mary Steventon 1922–43 and, possibly the most well-known of all during the '50s and '60s, Frank and Renee Fearns. The pub is still going strong 131 years after it was established by Arron Baggott in about 1871. (*T.J.H. Price*)

The Union Cross, 2 Oldbury Road, Greets Green, *c.* 1980, Albert Booker the licensee. Early records show that in 1834 a small brewery existed at the rear of this pub when the property was owned by John Wood. In 1884 William Bowen became the new proprietor, beginning a family association with these premises which lasted into the early 1940s. Doris Annie Booker was the last licensee prior to the pub's closure on 4 April 1984. (*T.J.H. Price*)

The Dunkirk Inn, 8 Whitehall Road, Greets Green, photographed in July 1968 when Raymond Swinson held the licence. In 1900 Charles Darby converted part of seventeenth-century Dunkirk Hall, which he had purchased from the late Alderman Reuben Farley's executors, into the inn pictured above. At the time of its closure on 5 January 1977 Michael Roberts was the licensee. (*Alan Price*)

A 'public house' tableau presented by the White Swan, Vernon Street, Greets Green, pictured here before joining the May 1937 coronation day parade around the streets of West Bromwich. (*Brenda Mackay*)

Greets Green Bowling Club presentation dinner Whitehall Tavern, Whitehall Road, *c.* 1954. Back row, left to right: Bill Ruston, Horace Scragg, Walter Griffiths, -?-, Bill Whitehouse, Sid Fletcher, Jack Heath, Billy Cooper, Mable Carter, Fred Leeson, -?-, Ted Carter (licensee), Jack Wherton, -?-, -?-, Horace Silwood, Irence Silwood, Bett Whitehouse, Sam Whitehouse, Jess Bowen. Left table: Cyril Rushton, -?-, ? Gould, ? Hodnett, Bella Withers, Billy Bishop, Tom Whitehouse, John Jacks, Mary Jacks, -?-, Zayer Wright. Right table: Emily Wherton, -?-, Jack Newell, Billy Haines, ? Nicholls, -?-, Tom Nicholls, -?-, -?-, ? Howells, Violet Page, -?-, Sid Page, Sam Birch, Arthur Bowen. (*Sheila Whitehouse*)

The White Swan Inn, 17 Vernon Street, Greets Green, *c.* 1931. Built in about 1870, the inn was run by William and Christiana Roberts for a total of twenty-eight years from 1922 to 1950. Sidney Ramsbottom was the last licensee when it closed in 1962 and also the first in its replacement, the Jolly Sailor, Oldbury Road, which opened on 14 June 1962. From left to right: William 'Caggy' Roberts, Bill Green, Alfred Marsh, William Roberts Jnr, Bill Bevan, John Roberts. (*Brenda Mackay*)

A harvest festival display in the bar of the White Swan, Vernon Street, Greets Green, *c.* 1950. Following these annual pub events the produce was usually auctioned and the money raised given to local charities. From left to right: Jack Joyce, William Roberts, -?-, Herbert Gadd, Freddy Smith. (*Brian Roberts*)

The Eight Locks public
house next to the Walsall
Canal at Ryders Green
Road, July 1968. An early
licensee was William Hale,
who kept the pub from
1868 until 1894. When
this photograph was taken
however, the landlord was
William Austwick.
According to local legend
Jack Judge is said to have
given the first public
performance of 'It's a long
way to Tipperary' in this
pub. (*Alan Price*)

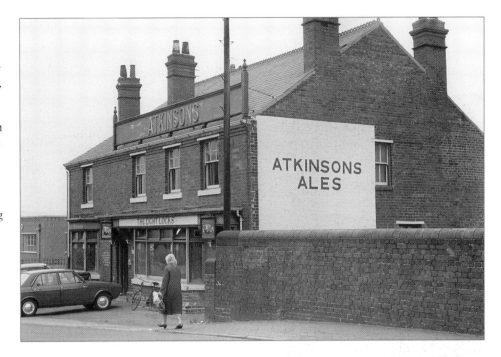

Thomas Harris, licensee of the Fox & Goose, 157 Greets Green Road, has his name prominently displayed above the
entrance to these premises. His wife Louisa stands on the left, *c.* 1910. The pub, which had remained in the Harris
family for fifty-six years since it was opened in 1870, was replaced around 1935 by the more modern present-day
building. (*T.J.H. Price*)

The Bush Inn, Wood Lane, Greets Green, *c.* 1949. These premises were erected in about 1936 replacing an older building dating back to around 1845. Successive members of the Pugh family were the first licensees, followed by Richard Jesson in 1865. Five years later George Darby bought the property which in 1895 passed to his son Charles, soon to become the proprietor of Darby's Brewery. The reputation of the Bush for beer quality and high standards reached its peak during 1943–51 under the management of Nancy and Harry Reynolds. (*Iris Reynolds*)

Greets Green Liberal Club, Whitehall Road, children's Christmas party committee, *c.* 1965. Back row, left to right: Sam Whitehouse (club steward), Gwen Copper, Cilla Burgess, Edna Scragg, Horace Scragg, Alice Kirkpatrick, Horace Burgess, Jack Kirkpatrick. Front row: Maud Copper, Bett Whitehouse, Muriel Smith, Bill Whitehouse, Arthur Sheldon. (*Sheila Whitehouse*)

The Old Crown Inn,
9 Sheepwash Lane, Great
Bridge, pictured here in
August 1968 while
under the management
of Lilian May
Shakespeare, the pub's
longest-serving licensee.
Charles Stamps is
recorded as being the
first landlord in 1865,
followed by Henry
Harper twenty years
later. (*Alan Price*)

The Dudley and District Federation of Pigeon Flying Clubs, Greets Green Branch, presentation dinner, Bush Inn, Wood Lane *c.* 1949. In front of the curtain, left to right: Joe Shakespeare, Jim Hughes, Harry Reynolds (licensee), Phil Payne, Bill Bates. Among those on the third table from the left: Joe Walker Snr, Joe Pincher, Tommy Smith, David Burton, Ray Skidmore, Barbara Skidmore, John Hughes. Fourth table: Joe Walker Jnr, Jim Powell, Norman Mayne, Geoff Mayne, Jim Jones, Mrs Walker Snr, Grace Walker, Harold Walker, Les Mosely. Behind the bar, left to right: Nancy Reynolds, Dolly Pearce, Maud Harley. (*Iris Reynolds*)

The Queen's Head, 93 Cophall Street, Great Bridge, *c.* 1967, when Horace Holden was the licensee. These premises opened on 5 January 1961 as a replacement for the well-known 'Tommy Wright's' Queen's Head pub, previously situated in nearby Horton Street. The building pictured here survived for just thirty-six years before being demolished on 15 August 1997, Glynis Carol Bennett being the last licensee. (*Andrew Maxam*)

The Royal Oak, 261 Whitehall Road, July 1968. The first mention of these premises was made in 1854 when Alfred Kendrick was landlord. However, by 1872 he had become a lime and coal merchant at Greets Green Wharf and a partner in the firm of Kendrick & Wooldridge, Ironfounders, Brickhouse Foundry, Great Bridge. Around the time of this picture the pub's licensees were Ann and Ted Penny. (*Alan Price*)

With beer bottles in hand and a further supply in their pockets, members of the Greets Green British Legion, Cape Street, prepare to board Dickie Horton's coach for a Sunday morning breakfast run, *c.* 1955. Left to right: Bill Hickingbottom, Jim Dugmore Dan Lawrence, -?-, Tommy Dugmore, Tom Bradley, -?-, Arthur Richards. (*Sam Price*)

The annual children's Christmas party held at Greets Green Liberal Club, Whitehall Road, *c.* 1963. Front row, left to right: Julie Arnold, Mark Copper, -?-, Mark Whitehouse, Jackie Jones, Heather Sheldon, Jenny Spooner, Linda Martin, June Burgess holding Gary Burgess, -?-, -?-. Among those behind: Michael Smith, Deborah Hodgkisson, Ian Fisher, Steven Arnold, Graham Burns, Gary Arnold, Carol Bowen, Elaine Fisher, Ann Kirkpatrick, Maureen Smith, Arthur Sheldon, Roland Coates, Tony Martin, Steven Pedley. (*Sheila Whitehouse*)

The bar of the Rose & Crown in Cape Street, Greets Green, *c.* 1964, showing from left to right: Jack Hadley, Edith Hadley, Bill Spooner, Iris Spooner. According to *Kelly's Directory* of 1880 licensee Joshua Bailey occupied half of these premises (No. 54), then known as 'The Crown', while next door at No. 56 was Thomas Harrison, haberdasher. Jack Hadley kept the pub from 1953 until 8 February 1979, when Keith Moorcroft became the licensee. (*Horace Burgess*)

The *c.* 1930 prize-winning Rose & Crown (Cape Street) jazz band pictured on 'The Mansion' in front of Grout and Sand Streets, Greets Green with, in the front row, their conductor Bill Edwards holding the Samson Cup. Among those in the sixth row: Sam Whitehouse. Fifth row: Jack Dyke, Tom Dyke, Bill Whitehouse. Fourth row: George Yates (the jester). Third row: Violet Parkes, Ethel Glover. (*David Dyke*)

Chapter Three
The Sporting Scene

Players and officials of Great Bridge Football Club pictured during the 1920/1 season. This photograph represents an interesting development in the sporting history of Great Bridge when the area apparently established its own football club through the support of Teddy Fisher, proprietor of a local confectionery shop. The team was managed by Frank Moreton and had its home ground at the back of the Seven Stars pub in Tame Road. Walter Silwood Snr is standing between two seated players on the right of the goalkeeper. (*Walter Silwood*)

Possibly the last picture ever taken of Church Army Social FC after becoming joint holders, along with Shamrock Rovers, of the Handworth League's Albion Shield during the 1954/5 season. Sadly, the Social Centre, seen here in the background and known locally as the 'Tin Hut', closed in 1957. Back row, left to right: -?-, George Shingleton, Bernard Roberts, Archie Reed, Jimmy Gittins, -?-, Brian Pace, Freddy Turton. Front row: Dennis Nock, Jess Bowen, Derek Freeman, Frank Dudfield, Donald Reed, Geoff Fellows. (*Frank Dudfield*)

Elwell FC, from Elwell Street, Great Bridge, pictured during their 1963/4 season when they became champions of the Handsworth League's Premier Division. Back row, left to right: Michael Stanford, Billy Harris, Peter O'Dea, Ken Hunter, Roy Smith, David Fisher, Bruce Carter. Front row: Lawrence Woods, Billy Hughes, John Nicholls, Ray Newell, Graham Brookes. (*T.J.H. Price*)

Greets Green Prims youth FC, 1955/6 season, league champions and winners of the Smethwick League's Grove and Tividale youth cups. Back row, left to right: David Nightingale, David Dyke, Tony Welch, Keith Slater, John Lewis, Jimmy Cox, Brian Harley, Tommy Meek, Ron Bates, Brian Aston, Tony Moore, Jack Dyke, Tom Dyke. Front row: Colin Whitehouse, Billy Smith, Terry Talbot, Ron Bowen, Trevor Woolley, Graham Dyke. (*David Dyke*)

Greets Green Prims FC, members of the Smethwick League, photographed at The Hawthorns before their Britannia Cup final success of season 1959/60. Back row, left to right: David Nightingale, Billy Todd, Howard Holland, Harold Lester, John Ainge, John Harris, Billy Richards, Joe Dyke. Front row: Fred Reed, Sid Day, Harry Bird, Stan Bates, Arthur Biston. (*David Dyke*)

Church Army Social FC, Greets Green, seen here before their West Bromwich League Division 1 match with West Bromwich Hostels at Wilford Road, 1949/50 season. Back row, left to right: Derek Hodgkisson, John Fox, George Hunt, Bernard Roberts, Ron Jukes, Bernard Morris, Tom Harper, Stan Lewis, Stan Bates, Harry Bird. Front row: Jack Goodwin, Jess Bowen, Len Holloway, Arthur Hartshorne, Ray Wyant. (*Vera Morris*)

Toll End Wesley FC, members of the Wolverhampton Amateur League Division 1, outside their chapel on 19 January 1952. Back row, left to right: Ernie Court, Frank Bradley, Joe Mann, Ronnie Walker, Tom Cartwright, Terry Hodgkins, Jimmy Darling, Jack Bache, Dennis Baker, -?-, Ray Bolton, Jack Cartwright, Raymond Walker. Front row: Ernie Willis, Reg Kramer, Walter Walker, Vernon Danks, Jack Gray. (*Brian Walker*)

Greets Green (Sandhole) Mission FC on 'The Nelson', 1921/2. This Evangelical Mission, which closed around 1928, was situated near the junction of Cape Street and Dunkirk Street (later Avenue). Its leader, Joseph Raybould, was a local rag-and-bone man who plied his trade around the area aboard a donkey and cart. Back row, extreme right: Joseph Ingram. Sam Raybould and Walter Taylor are in the middle row, fifth and sixth from the left, while Bill Holmes is first from the left, front row. (*Brenda Cook*)

Pictured in Victoria Park, Tipton, *c.* 1956 are West Bromwich League members New Road Methodist FC from Great Bridge. Back row, left to right: Malcolm Brewer, Roger Thornhill, David Higgs, Alan Breedon, Don Sheldon, Alan Smith. Front row: Alan Groucutt, Douglas Smith, William Cox, Bob Jones, Tom Wright. (*Bob Jones*)

Heath Rovers FC, members of the Wednesbury League, pictured behind the Old Crown public house in Toll End Road, Great Bridge, *c.* 1953. Back row, left to right: Walter Bevan, Stan Harvey, Ken King, Stan Cope, Terry Powell, Fred Powell, -?-. Front row: William Stanley, ? Marsh, Alf Powell. (*Ken King*)

Queens Head Rovers FC, better known as 'Tommy Wrights', pictured at the top of Cophall Street, Great Bridge, following their victory in the Handsworth League's Albion Shield final played on Tuesday 7 April 1931 at The Hawthorns. Back row, left to right: John 'Tricky' Walker, -?-, -?-, -?-, Harry Reed, -?-. Middle row: Herbert Evans Snr, Philip Franks, -?-, Tommy Wright, Jim Lycett, -?-, -?-, Tommy Dugmore, Tom Stokes, Billy Clifton. Front row: -?-, -?-, Albert Dunn, -?-, Herbert Evans Jnr, -?-, Albert Walker, -?-. (*Ron Dugmore*)

Greets Green Wesley FC, winners of the Handworth League's Albion Shield, *c.* 1922. The boy climbing over the fence, pictured right, is Cyril Davies who in 1935 joined West Bromwich Albion FC. Back row, left to right: Harry Cowley, Tom Powell, Alderman John Davies, Bob Jones Snr, Joe Davies. Third row: -?-, -?-, -?-, ? Draper, ? Smith, John Skeldon, Walter Shirley, -?-, Fred Lester. Second row: -?-, -?-, Sam Richards. Front row: -?-, -?-, John Davies Jnr, -?-, 'Baldy' Foster, ? Richardson, Jess Parkes. (*Bob Jones*)

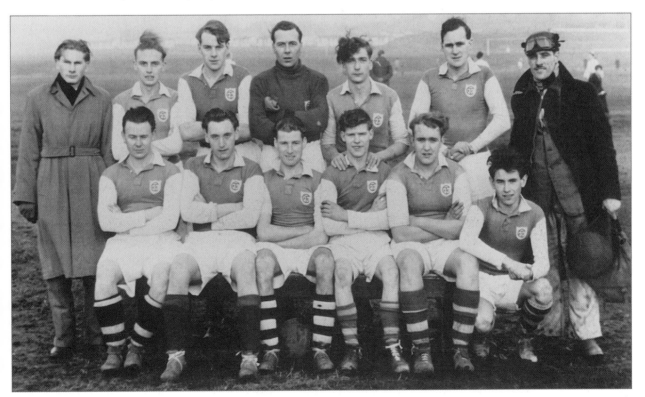

Conex-Terna FC (Great Bridge), Division 1 members of the West Bromwich League, pictured on Greets Green 'Rec', *c.* 1952. Back row, left to right: -?-, Reg Aston Ron Tedstone, -?-, -?-, Joe Evans, Les Wilkes. Front row: Cliff Davies, Harold Saunders, Frank Holland, -?-, -?-, -?-. (*Ron Tedstone*)

Pictured at The Hawthorns are St Paul's FC of Golds Hill who in 1961 were West Bromwich League Division 1 champions, winners of the Albion Shield and joint holders of the league's Knock-Out Cup. Back row, left to right: Brian Warner, Ron Timmins, -?-, George Allen, -?-, Fred Furnival, Cliff Andrews, Bill Hollyhead. Front row: Fred Perry, Tommy Bromley, Norman Glover, Joe Williams, Jim Andrews, Jim Hughes, John Harrison, Peter Osell. (*Joe Williams*)

Greets Green pub team Union Celtic FC of the West Bromwich League face the camera on Greets Green 'Rec' during the 1955/6 season. Back row, left to right: Gordon Longhurst, Alan Richards, Ray Guise, Arthur Evans, Ron Evans, Gerry Maddox. Front row: Billy Piper, George Pritchard, John Fellows, Gordon Lily, Stan Sharman. (*George Pritchard*)

Robinson Brothers FC of Ryders Green, Division Three champions and Phoenix Cup winners in the West Bromwich League 1955/6 season. Back row, left to right: Ron Massey, Ernie Griffiths, -?-, Les Crowe, Arthur Prince, Alan Brierley, Brian Pace, Alf Rooke. Front row: Dennis Price, Joe Howes, Hugh Gallimore, Gordon Cooper, Len Edwards, Alan Riley. (*Joseph Howes*)

St Paul's FC, Golds Hill, *c.* 1953, winners of a local challenge cup donated by Hill Top newsagent Mr H. Edwards. Back row, left to right: Bill Hollyhead, Len Beasley, Harold Grice, -?-, Maurice Cooper, Maurice Thorpe, Thomas Barnett. Middle row: Terry Woodcock, Len Whitehouse, Ted Jackson, Walter Sharman, Joe Williams. Front row: Ken Stokes, Alan Billingham. (*Keith Jackson*)

Warwickshire & West Midlands Alliance side Swan Village United FC pictured before their Aston Villa Cup semi-final clash with Stone Cross FC, *c.* 1967. Back row, left to right: Martin Philpott, Malcolm Johnson, George Lee, Paul Brownhill, Dougie Bartlett, Graham Mole, Barry Jukes, Colin James, Brian Osell, Ron Woodhall. Front row: ? Woodhall, Peter Osell, Dean Osell, David Philpott, Trevor Wilding, Brian Hickman, Harold Devey, Paul Osell, Jim Everett. (*Joyce Partridge*)

Handsworth League side Hawthorn Juniors FC from Golds Hill, season 1940/1, winners of the T.R. Fardell Cup, the League Division 1 Shield and the Arthur Turner Memorial Cup. Back row, left to right: Arthur Bednam, Harold Bird, Ernie Lawley, Sam Jeavons, Philip Burgess, Ivor Williams, Gilbert Williams, Tom Evans. Front row: Ray Attwood, Harry Hughes, Charlie Evans, Horace Ball, Arthur Evans. (*Molly Williams*)

Toll End Labour Club FC, winners of the Whitehouse Cup in the Tipton League, *c.* 1957. Back row, left to right: Alf Hickman, George Emms, Jim Harris, Jack Hodgkins, Fred Bowen, Ron Stanton, Wilf Vale. Front row: Alan Nicklin, Ron Russell, Cyril Jones, Ron Webb, Philip Partridge, Sid Shaw. (*Harry Pritchard*)

Swan Village FC, winners of the Walsall Conduits Cup in the West Bromwich Sunday League, 1955/6. The club was formed in 1955 but disbanded in 1960 having been champions of Division 1 on two occasions and twice winners of the Walsall Conduits Cup. Back row, left to right: Peter Walkerdine, Fred Tillison, Harry Scott, Ernie Willis, Bill Timmins, Joe Tillison, Derek Stanley, Frank Holloway, Harry Grainger, -?-. Front row: Gordon Hill, David Willis, Stan Carter, Ray Carter, Bill Hill. (*Gordon Hill*)

Kingfisher FC from Charles Street, Great Bridge, pictured after finishing fifth in Division 15 of the Birmingham Works AFA 1949/50. They won the Sir Evelyn Cecil Shield that season by defeating A.E. Griffiths FC 4–3 in the final. Back row, left to right: Ken Watton, Harry Cope, Stan Yates, Fred Parton, Gerry Maddox, Stan Sharman, Eddie Gill. Front row: Arthur Knowles, Tommy Morris, Tommy Poulton, Sammy Poulton. (*Stan Sharman*)

Wellington Tube FC, Great Bridge, members of the Birmingham Works AFA, pictured at The Hawthorns after defeating Ratcliffs (GB) 2–1 in the final of the Albion Shield, 1949/50 season. Back row, left to right: Fred Randle, Ron Markham, Arthur Cartwright, Bill Randle, Frank Adams, -?-, Les Gregory, -?-, Albert Markham. Front row: Ray Markham, Teddy Weston, Jacky Burns, Walter Sims, Ernie Shaw. (*Doris Smith*)

Birmingham Works AFA outfit, Walsall Conduits FC pictured in about 1941 on their sports ground facing Brickhouse Lane, Great Bridge. In the background is an unusual view of Swan Village gas tank painted in wartime camouflage colours. Back row, left to right: Jack Shuke, Reuben Cresswell, Ernie Barlow, Jim Fullwood. Henry Delicott, Freddy Preston, -?-, -?-, Ernie Phillips. Front row: Tom Williams, Arthur Cole, Arthur E. Millard, Joe Evans, William Whalley, Teddy Phillips, Stan Phillips. (*Arthur Cole*)

Walsall Conduits FC, Dial Lane, who finished third in Division 2 of the West Bromwich League 1973/4 season. Back row, left to right: Chris Hughes, Bill Baker, Mick Gaglihardy, David Hardin, John Bromley, Kevin Hogan, Peter Hill, John Millard, Arthur Cole. Front row: David Carder, Michael Price, Brian Baker, John Whitehouse, Geoff Price, Keith Hardin, David Wilson. (*Arthur Cole*)

Greets Green Prims FC, winners of the Smethwick League's Britannia Cup in the 1945/6 season, pictured in front of the Rose & Crown pub in Cape Street. Back row, left to right: Joe Dyke, Walter Smith, Sam Bird, Joe Leatherland, -?-, Jim Rose, Bob Jones, -?-, Peter Higgs. Front row: Gordon Dyke, Maurice Cartwright, Tom Fellows, Jack Leadington, -?-. (*Jim Rose*)

Greets Green Prims FC, winners of the Handworth League's T.R. Fardell Cup, 1926/7 season. Back row, left to right: David Round, Billy Shelley, Billy Hirons, Reg Powell, ? Evans. Third row: -?-, -?-, Steve Millington, Fred Howes, Jim Cowley Snr. Second row: Ernie Fox, Billy Richardson (WBA), Jack Ralph, Ernie Fellows, -?-. Front row: Arthur Denny, ? Thompson, -?-, Jim Cowley Jnr, Billy Bevan, ? Thompson, Walter Taylor. (*David Dyke*)

Customers of the White Swan in Vernon Street pictured at Greets Green 'Rec' before taking part in a charity football match with the Dunkirk Inn on Christmas Day, *c.* 1956. From left to right: -?-, Jack Goodwin, Alan Sinar, Benny Goodman, Bernard Roberts, Charlie Day, Frank Dixon, -?-, Brian 'Buster' Roberts, Ray Snape, George Barnett. (*Brian Roberts*)

Dunkirk Rovers FC, Greets Green, members of the West Bromwich Sunday League, 1959/60 season. The club was formed by George Shellard and George Lawley in 1957, mostly from employees of Thorntons Garage in Dunkirk Avenue. Back row, left to right: Frank Long, Charlie Brooks, Terry Jones, John Walker, Bill Walters, Joe Jones. Front row: Geoff Whitehouse, Horace Burgess, Don Picken, Alan Brierley, Bill McCarthy. (*Horace Burgess*)

Brian Whitehouse, professional football player with West Bromwich Albion, Norwich City, Wrexham, Crystal Palace, Charlton Athletic and Leyton Orient. Born on 8 September 1935 at 132 Greets Green Road, Brian attended Greets Green and George Salter schools. After leaving school he briefly played for Vono Sports before becoming an amateur with West Bromwich Albion in April 1950. He signed professional forms for them in October 1952 and made his debut at Portsmouth in a 1–1 draw on 14 April 1956. Brian was a versatile forward who scored seventeen goals in forty-six first-team games for the 'Baggies', his appearances being restricted by the form of fellow professionals such as Ronnie Allen, Johnny Nicholls, Derek Kevan and Bobby Robson. He scored both goals, however, in the 2–2 FA Cup semi-final draw with Aston Villa in 1957 and was bitterly disappointed when Albion lost the replay 1–0. In the years following his transfer to Norwich City in 1960 for £7,000 Brian joined a number of football league clubs in a playing, coaching and managerial capacity and while at Arsenal guided their youngsters to victory in the 1971 FA Youth Cup final. Brian scored over 100 goals in more than 300 league and cup outings during his eighteen-year playing career. (*Sheila Whitehouse*)

Gilbert Williams, professional football player with West Bromwich Albion and Banbury Spencer. Born on 12 January 1925 at 10 Tasker Street, Gil attended Greets Green Infants and Junior, Harvills Hawthorn and Hill Top schools until the age of fourteen. Afterwards, while playing for Hawthorn Juniors, he was spotted by West Bromwich Albion who signed him as an amateur on 25 September 1943. He made his debut the same day in a wartime league game against Wolves at the Hawthorns where a crowd of 7,363 saw Albion win 4–1. In February 1944 he signed professional forms with the 'Baggies' but shortly afterwards was called up for national service. Following demobilisation he made his football league debut on 13 September 1947 in a second division away match at Luton Town, a 1–1 draw in front of 26,155 fans. Gil was a short, sturdy wing-half with a biting tackle and always displayed a vigorous approach to the game. In total he made thirty-seven first team appearances, seven league, two FA cup and twenty-eight in other matches during the Second World War. After a spell with Banbury Spencer FC (1949–51) he continued his playing career with Wellington Tube Works FC until retiring from the game in 1969, aged forty-four. (*Molly Williams*)

Norman Alfred Male, professional football player with West Bromwich Albion and Walsall, was born on 28 May 1917 at 89 Greets Green Road and educated at Greets Green Infants and Junior and Cronehills schools. As well as captaining West Bromwich schoolboys he played for Cromwell United and afterwards, while with Bush Rangers, signed amateur forms for West Bromwich Albion in November 1933. He became a professional with Albion in October 1934 and won a junior international cap for England in 1935. Norman was a tall, well-built right-back who was limited to just four first team appearances with Albion because there were so many other quality full-backs at the club. In May 1938 he was transferred to Walsall for £250 where, after being converted to left-back, he made 265 first team appearances, 184 of them in wartime fixtures. During these war years he also guested for his old club West Bromwich Albion. Norman was forced to retire from playing in August 1949 after sustaining an injury to his knee during a match against Millwall in November 1948, but he continued to work as a member of the ground staff at Fellows Park until 1975. He died in 1992, aged seventy-five. (*Tony Matthews*)

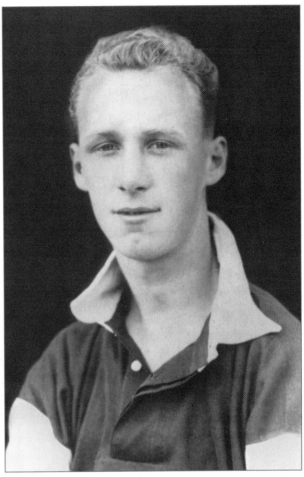

George Male, professional football player with Crystal Palace. Born on 18 May 1924 at 89 Greets Green Road, and brother of Norman Male, George was educated at Greets Green Infants and Junior and George Salter schools. His first junior club was Cordley Vic's and afterwards Hawthorn United when he left school in 1938. During the Second World War, while working and playing for Vono Ltd he had trials for Walsall and Leicester City, the latter club offering him a contract which he subsequently declined. However, when guesting for Walsall George was later spotted by Jack Lewis of Crystal Palace, the club for whom he eventually signed professional forms in the summer of 1945. George, a hard tackling and scheming inside forward, made his debut for the Glaziers on 25 August 1945 in a Division 3 South (Southern Region) 0–0 draw at home to Aldershot in front of a 7,000 crowd. During his stay at Selhurst Park he made fourteen appearances for the club, including five in the first team. In 1948, after a spell in the Royal Engineers, he resumed his previous occupation with Vono Ltd at Tipton for whom he continued playing until retiring from football in 1959. (*George Male*)

William James Roberts, a professional football player with Kidderminster Harriers, Flint Town and Cardiff City, was born at 41 Vernon Street, Greets Green on 20 January 1903, attending Greets Green Board School until the age of thirteen. In August 1919 Bill joined West Bromwich Albion as an amateur player before moving five years later to Kidderminster Harriers where he became a professional in May 1924. His next club was Flint Town from where he was transferred to Cardiff City in August 1928, making his football league Division 1 debut three months later on 17 November against Huddersfield Town in a 0–0 draw. A hard tackling left-back with a superb attitude towards the game he remained at Ninian Park for four seasons making 128 league appearances and scoring one goal. He was a virtual ever-present in the side and his only goal was a cracker, scored against Southampton on 16 November 1929 when Cardiff won 5–2. During 1932 Bill returned to the Midlands where he signed for Greets Green Wesley who at that time were members of the Worcestershire Combination. When his professional career ended he became a 'cropper' in the hot mill of Messrs J.B. & S. Lees Ltd, whom he joined on 5 September 1934. (*John Crooks*)

Ron Dugmore, professional football player with Wolverhampton Wanderers and Halesowen Town. Born on 7 April 1931 at 20 Cophall Street, Great Bridge, Ron attended Fisher Street and George Salter schools until the age of fourteen. After leaving school he played for Newtown Rangers FC before signing amateur forms for Wolverhampton Wanderers in 1946. Two years later, at the age of seventeen, he signed for the Wolves as a full-time professional with a weekly wage in the playing season of just £6. Ron was a player of great vision and as an attacking inside forward was always attempting to do something positive with the ball. Unfortunately his five-year period at Molineux also coincided with the emergence of players who were to become some of the great Wolves' forwards of the 1950s such as Peter Broadbent, Jimmy Mullen, Johnny Hancocks, Roy Swinbourne, Dennis Wilshaw and as a consequence almost all of his appearances were confined to the 'A' team, the one exception being a Central League game at Barnsley. In 1951, following his national service, Ron was transferred to Halesowen Town where he made 200 appearances scoring 139 goals, including eight in a 10–1 away win against Dudley Town. He retired from professional football in 1963. (*Halesowen Town FC*)

Prizefighter Bill Stimpson was born on 29 April 1901 at 37 Sheepwash Lane, Great Bridge, and later attended Fisher Street School until the age of thirteen. His first job was in an iron foundry, an occupation he continued until his retirement in 1972. He entered the boxing ring in the 1920s often fighting at catch-weight and on many occasions, when someone else's opponent failed to turn up, had two fights in one night. During his boxing career, which continued into the late 1930s, Bill's fighting title was 'The Pride of the Black Country'. After his marriage to Lily May Booker in 1926 they moved to Old Cross Street in Tipton where Bill attended the nearby Coppice Street Methodist Chapel. He eventually became a Lay Preacher and Trustee there while also joining the 5th Tipton Boys Brigade. In 1942 he completed a training course with the Staffordshire Youth Committee for leaders of boys clubs and reached the grade of Boys Brigade Captain in 1944. When the Coppice Street Mission closed in 1965 he continued his preaching and Boys Brigade work at Summerhill Methodist chapel which later closed around 1980. After devoting a lifetime's work to the good of the local community Bill passed away in December 1985, aged eighty-four. (*Margaret Tromans*)

International angling champion Bob Tromans was born at 77 New Road, Great Bridge, on 6 July 1936. He attended Great Bridge and Ocker Hill schools until 1951 when he began a thirty-two year career as a core maker at Coneygre Foundry Ltd, Tipton. Bob began fishing when only four years old and by the age of twelve was taking part in competitions. He joined the open fishing circuit in 1956 winning numerous contests such as the River Taff and the Great Ouse championships. Following his marriage to Margaret Stimpson in 1960 he had the distinction of being a member of the Kidderminster team which won the national championship of 1964 and, as part of the Coleshill team, secured the trophy again in 1972 and 1974. International honours followed when he was selected to represent England in the 1974 world angling championship in Belgium. Although the team was unsuccessful, Bob was the only member of the English contingent to win one of the twelve individual medals. In 1983, following his many appearances on radio and television, he decided to open a fishing tackle shop at Horseley Heath, which in 1993 was relocated to 135 Toll End Road. (*Margaret Tromans*)

Wellington Tube Works cricket team of *c.* 1947 at their sports ground in Elwell Street, Great Bridge. Back row, left to right: Edith Corbett, Walter Sims, Elisha Richards, Tom Austin, Victor Sims, Jacky Burns, Arthur Agger, Tom Corbett, Front row: William Stampe, ? Lawley, John Parry, Ken Lloyd, Harry Richards, Fred Markham, Bill Smith. Kneeling: Dorothy Richards. (*Jeffrey Stampe*)

The Wellington Tube Works cricket team at their Elwell Street sports ground, *c.* 1955. Back row, left to right: Tom Corbett, -?-, Walter Sims, Elisha Richards, Ken Lloyd, Harry Richards, Tommy Burns, -?-, Jacky Burns. Front row: Victor Sims, John Parry, Arthur Agger, Fred Markham. (*Walter Sims*)

Farley Park bowling green, Whitehall Road, *c.* 1905, with the park keeper's lodge in the background. This sporting activity is a particular favourite in the Greets Green area and has continued to be played here throughout the park's 111-year history. (*T.J.H. Price*)

Ratcliffs (GB) Ltd bowling team, league champions and winners of the Free Press Cup, 1958. Back row, left to right: -?-, Fred Butler, Harry Trotman, Jack Isherwood, Ray Bolton, -?-, Ernie Simms, George Arnold, George Worsey, J. Webb, Edward Ratcliff, David Watton. Middle row: Sammy Richardson, David Bowen, Bill Tansley, Sam Carter, Dick Jukes, Dick Penn, Sid Clarke, Bert Talbot, Bill Smith, Tom Lloyd, Arthur Watson, Peter Ratcliff. Front row: John Joesbury, Bert Bennett, Mo Cooper, Jimmy Jacks, Martin Ratcliff, Fred Kelly, Joe Hickman, Alf Terrett, Stan Ashwood. (*Fred Kelly*)

The Stork Bowling Club, Great Bridge, with the five trophies won during their successful 1966 season. Back row, left to right: Charlie Bromley, Jim Partridge Jnr, Tom Boulton, John Jacks Jnr, Sam Boxley, Jack Stevens, Charlie Williams, Tom Sharman, George Moore, Dennis Moseley, Harold Shingleton, Harry Parkes, Tom Davies, Jack Shaw, Harold Allen, Mick Homer. Front row: Bill Woodcock, John Jacks, Sam Nicholas, Albert Timmins, Jim Partridge, Ernie Lees, Harold 'Curly' Winsper, Albert Winsper, Peter Butler. (*Tom Sharman*)

Bowling league champions and cup winners Walsall Conduits of Dial Lane line up to be photographed, *c.* 1959. Back row, left to right: Bill Foley, Joe Evans, Arthur Cole, Albert Rotten, Joe Billington, Eric Dixon, Bill Dixon, Bill Jones. Front row: Eddie Phillips, Joshua Churchman, Jimmy Jones, Bill Evans, Jim Wheatley. (*Joshua Churchman*)

With Brickhouse Lane in the background, Walsall Conduits bowling team poses for a photograph, *c.* 1950. Back row, left to right: Arthur Handley, Howard Matchett, Jimmy Jones, George Billington, George Upton, Jim Smith, Fred Griffiths. Front row: ? Lovett, Tom Lovett, Jim Wheatley, Joe Holloway, Billy Evans, Tom Wheatley, -?-, ? Griffiths. (*Louie Truby*)

Winners of the Free Press Cup, Greets Green Bowling Club members are seen here with the trophy in Farley Park, *c.* 1964. Back row, left to right: Walter Griffiths, Arthur Sheldon Jnr, Arthur Sheldon Snr, Tom Bowen, Sid Page, Ken Arnold, Sam Whitehouse, Tom Nicholls, Jack Kirkpatrick. Front row: Bill Whitehouse, Jess Bowen, Ron Fox, Horace Scragg, Joe France. (*Sheila Whitehouse*)

Club members in the snooker room of Greets Green British Legion, Cape Street, *c.* 1955. The building was demolished in 1988 and a bungalow now occupies part of the site, near the Rose & Crown public house. From left to right: John Howes Snr, Jimmy Fellows, Rose Yates, Mary Meredith, Wilf Knight, -?-, Albert Jeavons, Herbert Hunt, -?-, Charlie Copper. (*Horace Burgess*)

Wellington Tube Works table tennis team and officials outside the offices in Brickhouse Lane, Great Bridge, following their West Bromwich League championship and five cup successes of 1939. Back row, left to right: Cyril Turner, Walter Sims, Alf Wellings, Herbert Howell, Tom Corbett, Joe Smith, David Hopkins, Fred Yates. Front row: Jack Tolley, Ernie Ledbury, Douglas W. Turner, Herbert Glover, Alf Tolley. (*David Hopkins*)

Chapter Four
Chapel & Church

The war memorial in St Peter's Church, Whitehall Road, Great Bridge, following the unveiling and dedication by the Bishop of Stafford, Dr H.C. Crawford, on Wednesday 2 November 1921. The oak mural tablet bears the names of over 140 parishioners and members of the congregation who lost their lives in the First World War. The wall above was painted by Mr F.A. Jackson of London and depicts the risen Christ surrounded by ascending angels. Around 1985, during the incumbency of the Revd Paul Lockett, the memorial was removed and relocated to the rear of the church. (*Philip Evans*)

'Evergreen' Ivy May Round was born on 27 November 1915 at 32 Greets Green Road to parents Louisa and David Round, her father being a local Methodist Lay Preacher. She attended Greets Green Board School before finding employment with the Albion Spring Co. in Oldbury Road at the age of fourteen. In March 1933, having been associated with Greets Green Primitive Methodist Church since a babe in arms, Ivy became primary Sunday School Superintendent and church organist. The same year she also began writing and producing the now famous concert parties and pantomimes which her father named 'The Evergreens' after her own name, Ivy, an evergreen. Following closure of Greets Green PMC in 1958 she, and part of the congregation, moved to the Methodist church in Great Bridge Street where she continued her work with renewed vigour, supported by new Newfoundland husband Frank Hancock, whom she had married in 1955. In 1983, 'The Evergreens' 50th year, Ivy and her daughter Anne were invited to meet the Queen and Princess Diana at Buckingham Palace in recognition of her outstanding charitable work in the local community. Both Ivy and 'The Evergreens' are still going strong and, together with past and present performers, will celebrate their 70-year association in 2003. (*Ivy Round-Hancock*)

Mary Allway, at the age of only fourteen, the 1935 Carnival Queen of St Peter's Church, Whitehall Road, Great Bridge, with her attendant Milly Thomas on the vicarage lawn. The second of three children born to Annie and Captain Willougby Allway, Mary resided at the Church Army Social Centre in Whitehall Road with her two brothers, Bill and David. The family had arrived in the parish of St Peter's from Colchester in Suffolk during the depression of 1926 and immediately threw themselves enthusiastically into the work of caring for the local people of Great Bridge and Greets Green. Her father Captain Allway was also instrumental in providing leisure activities at the social centre during the evenings and at weekends, while her mother Annie helped with the running of the Mothers Union. After attending St Peter's, Greets Green and Cronehills schools Mary found employment in 'Earthquake Man', John J. Shaw's pawnshop at 129 New Street, West Bromwich, before volunteering for the Land Army in 1941. During these early years she was also involved with the Brownies and is still active today in local charitable work. (*Mary Allway*)

Greets Green Primitive Methodist Church Carnival Rose Queen, Miss Joan Smith, with her entourage in Whitehall Road following the crowning ceremony held in Farley Park bandstand, 1950. From left to right: -?-, Joan Thompson, Maureen Cartwright, Valerie Ives, Mary Howes, Barbara Arnold, Rita Jacks, Jean Thompson, Betty Jeavons, Joan Smith. (*Joan Howes*)

A production of *Cinderella* by 'The Evergreens' of Great Bridge Street Methodist church performed at Swan Village Methodist church, *c.* 1961. Back row, centre: Eadie Best, Alice Kirkpatrick. Fourth row; John Manders, Keith Stubbs, Michael Vaughan, Peter Best. Third row: Robert Edwards, John Fereday, -?-, Steven Edwards, Sid Wright, Margaret Smith, Ann Kirkpatrick, Peter Tomlinson, Elizabeth Addis, Ivy Round. Second row: Jacqueline Bingham, ? Cook, Diane Williams, Patricia Asbury, Anne Round, Joan Howes, Jacqueline Best, Rona Cooke, John Morris, -?-. Front row: Leslie Bingham, -?-, -?-. (*Joan Howes*)

'The Evergreens' at Greets Green Primitive Methodist Church, Whitehall Road, performing the pantomime *Babes In The Wood*, 1945. Among those on stage: Minnie Arnold, Barry Hopson, Bob Arnold, Ivy Round, Ethel Round, Doreen Tandy, Brenda Arnold, Louisa Round, Marjorie Fieldhouse, Doreen Whitehouse, Jean Arnold, Dorothy Fellows, Ann Dyke, Geoff Povey, Gwenda Yates, Albert Caddick, Iris Howes, David Howes, Sid Tandy, John Howes, Betty Tandy, Howard Baker, Joan Smith, Sheila Whitehouse, Stan Dodd. (*Sheila Whitehouse*)

Miss Margaret (Peggy) Bridges, Greets Green Primitive Methodist Church Carnival Queen of 1951, pictured on her way to Farley Park bandstand where she was crowned by Mrs J.P. Howell of Hartlebury. Among her retinue are: Ann Bridges, Iris Roden, Maureen Cooksey, Pat Doughty, Pat Lees, Maureen Smith, Joan Smith, Beatrice Dodd, Hazel Jackson, Doreen Cox, Iris Howes, Dorothy Cooksey, Ivy Round, Sheila Doughty. (*Stanley Durden*)

Members of 'The Evergreens' concert party and youth club attend a joint 21st birthday party for Olive Spink and Geoff Povey at Greets Green Primitive Methodist Church, Whitehall Road, January 1952. Back row, left to right: -?-, Ken Welch, -?-, Douglas Winterborn, Chas Huggins, Gladys Grigg, Howard Parker, Norma Charlton, -?-, Jack Nicklin, Iris Howes, Brenda Beady, David Howes, Bill Downes, David Round. Front row: Joan Smith, Janet Reynolds, Iris Pridey, Jeanette Reynolds, Olive Spink, Geoff Povey, Mary Bevan, Hazel Jackson, Ivy Round, Anne Round. (*Ken Bayley*)

A gypsy tableau, one of the winners in the Greets Green Primitive Methodist Church carnival fancy dress competition held here in Farley Park, Whitehall Road, *c.* 1950. From left to right: Tony Welch, Brian Wallace, Gordon Brookes, Howard Baker. (*Ian Downes*)

Great Bridge Street Methodist Church present 'The Evergreens' performance of *Jack and the Beanstalk, c.* 1971. Back row, left to right: Margaret Tromans, Freda Braden, Stan Dodd. Third row: Ivy Round, Barbara Dando, Jean Fereday, -?-, ? Thompson, Fred Sabin, Anne Round, Vera Sabin. In the cow: Ian Day, David Coley. Second row: Paul Fereday, Sharon Bishop, -?-, -?-, Karen Coley. Front row: Michael Hood, Ian Sabin, -?-, Jackie Braden, Angela Tromans. (*Margaret Tromans*)

The cast of *Puss in Boots* performed by 'The Evergreens' of Great Bridge Street Methodist Church, *c.* 1979. Back row, left to right: Gail Westwood, Helen Vaughan, Jackie Braden, Julie Heath, Malcolm Heath, Gwen Heath, Irene Hood, Diane Whitehouse, Angela Heath, Ivy Round, Michael Vaughan. Middle row: Jane Vaughan, Louise Mayne, Gillian Heath. Front row: Margaret Tromans, Angela Tromans, Anne Round. (*Margaret Tromans*)

Great Bridge Street Methodist Church Sunday School Anniversary, *c.* 1947. Front row, left to right: Ken Lowe, Michael Cropper, Rose Bromley, Janet Bromley, Cynthia Clarke, Ann Burns, Shirley Bromley, Maureen Jinks, Raymond Jinks, Patrick Williams. Among those behind are: Dorothy O'Brien, Maurice Knight, Doreen Maul, Gary Ablrighton, Janet Downing, Tony Harris, June Taylor, Pam Coley, Janet Hubble, Olive Hickinbottom, Jim Harris, Hilda Clark, Nellie Harris, Joan Clark, Marion Howes, Gloria Sansome, Maureen Parry, Audrey Downing, Sheila Capewell, Doris Maul, Jean Rushton, Colin Maul. (*Marion Jinks*)

Flower girls and attendants to the queen forming part of the St Peter's Church carnival parade of 1946, pictured at Farley Park, Greets Green, before departure. Back row, left to right: -?-, -?-, Jean Stevens, June Cox, Kathy Law. Front row: Eileen Dunne, Vera Phillips, Vera Calloway, -?-, Jean Griffiths, Audrey Dunn, -?-. (*Audrey Siverns*)

Greets Green Wesleyan Church, Ryders Green Road, *c.* 1905. The building was erected in 1874 at a cost of £1,780, replacing an earlier structure dating from 1834. Following a Deed of Union in 1932 between the Primitive, Wesleyan and other Methodist churches, the name was changed to the present-day title of Ryders Green Methodist Church. The Wesleyan school, shown at the rear, was built in 1856 and is now primarily a day centre attached to the church. (*T.J.H. Price*)

Greets Green Primitive Methodist Church carnival parade showing the 5th West Bromwich Boys Brigade leading the way in Whitgreave Street, *c.* 1953. In the centre background can be seen the rear of Darby's Brewery with Greets Green schools to the right. Left to right: Ken Dunn, Geoff Stokes, Victor Makepeace, John Madden, Alan Udall, Michael Osborne, Peter Timms. (*Dennis Woodall*)

The 7th Tipton Scouts (Great Bridge) in the playground of Fisher Street School, June 1953. Back row left to right: John Richards, Terry Caswell, -?-, John Whitehouse. Fifth row: Leslie Martin, Eric Gorton, Eric Shelley, Norman Gill, Maurice Shelley, Harold Parton, Alan Roberts. Fourth row: Victor Grainger, Tony Patrick, John Lappage, Billy Edwards, Michael Penn, Patrick Williams, Tony Leach, -?-, ? Pugh, ? Fellows, Denis Griffiths. Third row: John Gutteridge, Rita Richards, Mary Turner, Iris Gill (Akela), Brenda Marsh, Wilf Jones. Second row: Kenneth Dean, -?-, John Fereday, -?-, -?-, -?-, -?-, John Whitehouse. Front row: Robert Gutteridge; Roy Niblett, -?-. (*Iris Gill*)

Class one winners of the Greets Green Primitive Methodist Church carnival fancy dress competition of 1951, 'The Weird Cheese', featuring from left to right: Ken Bayley, Jack Nicklin. (*Ken Bayley*)

Members of St Peter's Church bible class departing from Whitehall Road, Great Bridge, on an outing to the seaside, *c.* 1920. In the background, on the right, is the St Peter's Council School building, erected in 1866. (*Robin Pearson*)

St Peter's Church, Whitehall Road, Great Bridge, Sunday School Anniversary, *c.* 1927. Among the back row are: Milly Binger, Winnie Welch. Sixth row: Irene Taylor, Mary Stockley, Gladys Bell, Muriel Law. Fifth row: Doris Green, Ada Hollender, Beatrice Stokes, Tommy Harper. Fourth row: Violet Evans, Agnes Jeffries, Edna Heath, Adelaide George, Mabel Simcox, May Capewell. Third row: Dora Martin, Lily Jones, Edith Marsh, Edna Stockley, Marjorie Mills, Alice Lovell. Second row: Ena Dunn, Maud Porter, Maud Jarvis, Kathy Meek, Clara Copper, Gladys Davies. Front row: Mary Allway, Olive Dunn, Edith Churchman, Arthur Churchman, Billy Leddington, Edna Parsons. (*Ada Dyke*)

Children on the vicarage lawn of St Peter's Church, Whitehall Road before their carnival parade, *c.* 1935. Back row, left to right: Rose Palfreyman, Olive Meek, Alice Heath, -?-, Muriel Bevan, Mabel Mills, Gladys Wicket, -?-. Middle row: -?-, May Heath, Iris Stevens, -?-, Hetty Curtis, Brenda Beacham, Joyce Newell, -?-, Rene Beacham, Lottie Thomas, Madge Venables, Mary Barnett, -?-, -?-, -?-. Front row: Joe Curtis, Alma Broad, Mary Churchman, -?-, -?-, -?-, -?-, Eric Churchman. (*May Hirons*)

St Peter's Church vicarage, Whitehall Road, Great Bridge, *c.* 1902. Erected in 1898 by the Revd Henry Jesson, the building survived until 1980 when it was demolished and replaced by housing association flats. The name chosen for this new development was Lancelot Place, after the Revd Lancelot John Lamplugh who served the parish of St Peter for a record total of thirty-six years. (*T.J.H. Price*)

The official opening of St Peter's church hall in Whitehall Road, Great Bridge, on 17 June 1966 by Mrs B. Stratton, wife of the Archdeacon of Stafford, The Venerable Basil Stratton, who afterwards dedicated the building during a service conducted by the Revd Michael Pollit. Also attending the ceremony was the Mayor of West Bromwich, Councillor Joshua Churchman and his mother Clara Churchman, who was deputising for the Mayoress Mrs Violet Churchman. Councillor Churchman, whose family have always had strong links with St Peter's, was born almost opposite the new hall in Whitehall Road and attended the church school which had previously occupied the site. His mother Clara was for many years housekeeper to the Revd Lancelot J. Lamplugh, at the vicarage, which was also situated in Whitehall Road near the Churchmans' family home. Shortly after the opening, however, as a result of a disastrous fire at the church in November 1966, the new hall had to be used by the congregation for religious services, a situation which lasted for just over twelve months. Left to right: The Ven. Basil Stratton, Mrs Clara Churchman, Mrs B. Stratton, Councillor Joshua Churchman, Revd Michael Pollit. (*Joshua Churchman*)

The interior of the Methodist New Connection Church, New Road, Great Bridge, *c.* 1905. For seventy-six years this church stood on the corner of Mount Street and New Road until it was destroyed by enemy bombing in the early hours of 17 May 1941. Following this disaster and after a short period of worship at St Paul's Church, Dudley Port, a few services were held at the council schools in Great Bridge. The congregation then moved again and made a temporary home at the Early Morning Adult School in Toll End. As the war dragged on so the longing to go home became greater, until early in 1945 temporary repairs were carried out on the small schoolroom in Mount Street, thus enabling the congregation to return shortly afterwards. In 1955 a rebuilding campaign was launched with an objective of raising £30,000, which included £12,000 already available from collections, grants and a war damage payment of £9,000. The first part of the scheme was to build a new church hall on the site of the old, which was eventually opened and dedicated for worship on Saturday 21 September 1957. The rebuilding campaign was completed in 1971 when a new and modern church at last opened its doors to a joyous congregation. (*T.J.H. Price*)

Young ladies' anniversary practice at St Peter's Church, Whitehall Road, Great Bridge, *c.* 1941. Back row, left to right: Mary Gwinnett, Lily Phillips, Freda Turner, Jean Earp, Cynthia Boxley, -?-, Jean Barnett, -?-, Iris Mumford, -?-, -?-, Brenda Corbett, -?-, Vera Price. Middle row: Dorothy Davies, Joyce Phillips, Brenda Oliver, -?-, Pat ?, -?-, Margaret Langford, Joan Guy, -?-, Cynthia Tonks, -?-, Shirley ?, -?-, -?-. Front row: Vera Phillips, Eileen Dunn, -?-, -?-, -?-, Irene Law, June Richards, Joyce Law, -?-. (*Lily Phillips*)

The interior of St Paul's Church, Golds Hill, *c.* 1930, showing the recently installed electric lighting. The church began life in a mission centre at the Golds Hill Ironworks of John Bagnall & Sons in 1853 and was served by the firm's Chaplain, the Revd Francis Hutton. On Monday 6 September 1887 the present church building was consecrated with a parish of 4,000 assigned to it from St James at Hill Top. (*Alan Price*)

An interior view of Toll End Wesley Chapel during a Sunday School Anniversary service, *c*. 1947. Among the back row, left to right: Alf Powell, Irene Gibbs, Gladys Powell, Mabel Edwards, Tom Dunn, Mrs Oliver, Mary Humphries, Howard Oliver. Third row, third, fifth and eighth: Beryl Taylor, Beryl Payne, Beryl Price. Second row, first, fifth and seventh: Avril Brinsden, Margaret Haynes, Joan Baker. Front row: Barbara James, Audrey Hesson, Beryl Harrison, Freda Brinsden, Margaret Hill, -?-, Valerie Lewis, Pat James, -?-, Molly Harrison, -?-, June Davies, -?-, -?-. (*Beryl Hill*)

St Peter's Church festival procession, 1 May 1921, progressing along Ryders Green Road in the direction of Phoenix Street. On the skyline in the background can be seen Greets Green schools next to Darby's Brewery in Whitehall Road. (*St Peter's Church*)

Pictured outside Toll End Wesley Chapel during their anniversary celebrations, *c.* 1950, are back row, third from left: Margaret Davies. Third row, first, fourth and tenth from the left: Ann Shaw, Doreen Haynes, Pam Shaw. Second row, tenth from the left: Doreen Grainger. Front row: Florence Barrow, Judith Holmes, -?-, -?-, Barbara Elmore, -?-, -?-, -?-, -?-, -?-, Sheila Steventon, Pauline Price. (*Brenda Cook*)

A young people's class (Fireside Group) from Great Bridge Trinity Methodist Church pictured at the manse in Sheepwash Lane, *c.* 1943. Back row, left to right: Ben Dunn Snr, Ben Dunn Jnr, Mary Bellingham, Len Bates, Harold Parton, Beryl Onions, Joe Dudley, Beryl Douglas, Eric Shelley, Barbara Poole, Fred Taylor, Lily Dunn. Middle row: Doreen Print, Howard Spicer, Revd Harry F. Barker, Marjorie Barker, Gerald Bates, Iris Vanes. Front row: Cynthia Tonks, Dorothy Davies, Brenda Edwards, Edna Hodgetts. (*Iris Gill*)

This delightful picture of a concert party group was taken in 1917 on the vicarage lawn of Salem Church, Sheepwash Lane, Great Bridge. Left to right: Rose Bissell, Ivy Farrington, Annie Freeth, -?-, -?-, Beatrice Williams, ? Priest, ? Screen. (*Rose Ward*)

Great Bridge Trinity Methodist Church, Sunday School Anniversary, *c.* 1954. Back row, left to right: Ernie Walker, Dennis Carpenter, John Gutteridge, Wilf Jones, Les Martin, Doug Edwards, Ron Martin, Michael Cormell, Donald Randle, Billy Pearson, Maurice Barlow. Sixth row: Barbara Poole, Evelyn Barlow, Edna Reynolds, Doris Hall, Nellie Walker, May Whitehouse, Ethel Vanes, Florrie Wood, Annie Evans. Among others on the platform: Mary Vanes, Sheila Jones, Linda Hall, Linda Jeavons, Linda Hallmark, Josephine Wooldridge. (*Wilf Jones*)

Salem Congregational Church Sunday School anniversary parade, Sheepwash Lane, Great Bridge, June 1973. At the head of the procession is John Webb (left) and Manny Wright (right), while at the rear (left) is Fred Day, the Church Secretary. Standing on the corner of Salem Street, extreme right, is Peter Webb. (*Jim Walters*)

Ryders Green Methodist Church Sunday School Anniversary, *c.* 1947. Among those on the upper level are: Harry Summers, William Davies, Gilbert Davies, Ben Preston, Marie Hodgetts, Amy Pickford, John Davies, Phoebe Davies, Florence Preston, Ethel Richards, Ruth Jones. Lower level: Olive Treadwell, Margaret Lewis, Gwynneth Aston, Pat Moore, Sheila Price, Jean White, Gladys Aston, Mary Lewis, Marie Richards, Molly Stevens, Pauline Pugh, Doreen Boswell, Maureen Guest, Janet Reynolds, Hazel Markham, Pat Lawley, Pat Lewis, Thelma Price, Audrey Lawley. (*Trevor Lawley*)

Children and teachers of Salem Congregational Church Sunday School, Sheepwash Lane, Great Bridge, presenting a Sister Dora tableau which won second prize during the coronation celebrations of 12 May 1937. Back row, left to right: Gladys Whitehouse, Mary Stockle, Helen Adamson. Middle row: Tom Adamson, Joe Whitehouse, Irene Davies. Front row: Harry Hickinbottom, Barbara Shepherd. (*Gladys Ryles*)

'The Optimists' concert party Salem Congregational Church, Sheepwash Lane, Great Bridge, *c.* 1953. Back row, left to right: Arthur Webb, Alan Webb, Philip Franks, Peter Webb, Harry Priest, Michael Priest, Ernest Hyde, Geoff Brevitt. Middle row: Margaret Whitehouse, Claude York, Cliff Williams, Horace Parkes, Gordon Brevitt, Manny Wright, Douglas Brevitt, Len Markham, Arthur Furnevall. Front row: Dora Day, Mary Stockle, Brenda Stevenson, Jean Roberts, Sandra Seager, Brenda Whitehouse, Gladys Whitehouse, Kathy Barber, Brenda Williams, Cliff Ball. (*Annie Ball*)

Chapter Five
Schooldays

Tom Shaw, the Great Bridge 'lollipop man' attached to Fisher Street School, seen here outside Frederick and Edna Groom's menswear shop, *c.* 1964. He served the local community in this capacity for over ten years until his retirement in 1965. Tom, who lost an arm while serving in the First World War, was a great favourite with the children and would even accompany them on their school outings to the seaside. (*Monica Richards*)

Young pupils assemble for a class photograph in 1938 at Fisher Street School, Great Bridge. Back row, left to right: Jean Stanley, Tommy Allen (part hidden), Olive Baker, Betty Smith, Geoffrey Price, Jack Niblett, Edna Read, Cynthia Tonks, Edna Winterbourne. Middle row; Brenda Oliver, Brenda Stevenson, Hilda Law, Brenda Williams, Sylvia Johnson, Cynthia Boxley. Front row: Brian Dunkley, Christine Stampe, Lilian Wright, Ronald Dugmore, Elsie Price, -?-. (*John Stampe*)

Fisher Street School, *c.* 1936. Back row, left to right: Sheila Capewell, Sybil Price, Doreen Horton, Doris Boffie, Ruth Eaton. Third row: Edna Wild, Doris Fardell, Olive Daulman, Olive Bowen, Doreen Martin, Ann Heywood, Joan Bell. Second row: Nellie Aston, Dorothy Talbot, Sylvia Whitehouse, Beryl Cook, Irene Randle, Margaret Dean, Mary Beddows. Front row: Mary Hickinbottom, Edith Reid, Ida Sayce, -?-, Rosalie Wilkes. (*Edna Tromans*)

The nursery class at Fisher Street School, *c.* 1947, with May Poulton among those children on the left of the picture. Jennifer Evans is seated centre, while Brian Shenstone on the right is looking towards one of the teachers. (*Jennifer Evans*)

A large class of pupils at Fisher Street School, *c.* 1931. Back row, left to right: Doris Martin, John Houghton, -?-, Len Bates, Joe Morris, Sam Causer, Nel Stott, Doris Williams, Olive Randle, Pauline Price, Audrey Adams. Middle section: Brenda Homer, Doreen Ingram, Doris Niblett, Gwen Smith, Tommy Howes, George Parker, Oliver Gilbert, Edna Sims, Wilf Jones, Joe Price, Kathleen Smith, Gwen Niblett, Ida Sayce, Eileen Arnold, Rosalie Wilkes, Elizabeth Wright. Front row: Eric Wright, Arthur Jackson, Dennis Lewis. (*Doris Bunch*)

The annual outing from Fisher Street School, to Deganwy and Llandudno, *c.* 1948, showing pupils paddling in the sea accompanied by their teacher Miss Vera Bamford. Back row, left to right, Michael Kellas, -?-, Gloria Sansome. Front row: ? Martin, -?-, Janet Hubble, Ann Hickinbottom, Jim Powell, Vera Bamford, Dorothy Parsons, Janet Bromley, ? Best, Margaret Burton. (*Bertha Griffiths*)

Children from Fisher Street School with teacher Bob Bowles on the beach at Llandudno during their annual outing to the seaside, *c.* 1949. Back row, left to right: Michael Kennett, Brian Ruston, -?-, -?-, -?-, Peter Best, Margaret Markham, Janet Hubble, -?-, Beryl Martin, -?-, Cynthia Clarke, Arthur Crutchley. Front row, -?-, -?-, -?-, ? Best, Ann Burns, -?-. (*Bertha Griffiths*)

An infants class at Fisher Street School, *c.* 1946. Top left, from left to right: Michael Parker, Fred Reed, Sheila Boswell, Jean Fletcher, Beryl Devison, -?-, Ann Jones, Gwen Davies, Dorothy Bennett. Back row, right side: Gillian Parkes, Joseph Tedstone, Terry Nock. Sixth row: Shirley Bromley, Collin Simmonds, Jacqueline Pearson, Michael Cropper. Fifth row: John Martin, Iris Haycock, -?-, Gordon Fullwood. Fourth row: Dennis Stevens, Kathleen Downes, Jimmy Drummond, Valerie Smith. Third row: Rita Parkes, Raymond Jinks, Peter Coley, Irene Preece. Second row: ? Lowe, ? Lilley, Ann Amos. Front row: Brenda Brown, Wilf Stokes, Tony Nock, George Bullock. (*Shirley Mauldridge*)

Another Llandudno view of pupils from Fisher Street School, *c.* 1948. Back row, left to right: Ruby Fisher, Brenda Small, Ann Hodson. Front row: Ruth Stampe, Gloria Sansome, Flossie Cox. (*Bertha Griffiths*)

Children hard at work in an arts and crafts class at Fisher Street School, *c.* 1947. To the left of the radiator at the back of the class are Sheila Capewell and June Taylor. Centre: Marion Howes, Doreen Maull and Kathy Downes. Right foreground: Gary Albrighton. (*Sally Howes*)

A happy group of young ladies in the playground of Fisher Street School, *c.* 1935. Back row, left to right: Barbara Sheppard, Doreen Worley, Gwen Boughton, Irene Melia, Gwen Fardell, Aileen Mincher, Elizabeth Coley, Lily Flukes. Middle row: Marjorie Nock, Iris Vanes, Annie Henshaw, Irene Price, Joyce Price, Audrey Timmins, Iris Chadbourne. Front row, Brenda Jarvis, -?-, -?-, -?-, Dorothy Williams, Pauline Johnson. (*Irene Pitt*)

In the playground, pupils from Fisher Street School, 1938. Back row, left to right: Irene Walker, Marjorie Gilbert, Joyce Ore, Freda Turner, Vera Davies, Doreen Homer, Doreen Maloy, Margaret Parkes, Connie Venables, Margaret Llewellyn. Middle row: Vera Franks, Beryl Holland, Mary Markham, Leslie Johnson, Joyce Masters, Irene Stanley, Margaret Daulman. Front row: Howard Parker, Gerald Bates, -?-, Gordon Small, -?-, Fred Machin, Arthur Smith, Jim Harris. (*Joyce Ferrington*)

Pupils playing a game of 'oranges and lemons' to music from a nearby wind-up gramophone at Fisher Street School, *c*. 1946. Left to right: Rita Hennefer, Arthur Steventon, Reg Price, Freda Woodhall (part hidden), June Taylor, Derek Woodhall (part hidden), Barbara Tedstone, Jim Stevens, Doris Maull (part hidden), Maurice Beddows, Alan Fullwood, Pam Coley. (*Barbara White*)

A fishing trip to 'Tommy Wright's Fields' from the appropriately named Fisher Street School, *c.* 1952. Back row, left to right: Alice Toon, Pauline Morris, Pat Tillison, Josie Kennett, Billy Gale, Valerie Burns, -?-, John Whitehouse, Jean Rackham, Michael Aldritt, Maureen Morgan. Third row: Valerie Fletcher, Rita Dyke, Maureen Bailey, Irene Randle, John Allmark, Pat Davies, Christine Sowry, Judith Green, Derek Holden, Pauline Hall, Reg Cook. Second row: Terry Salt, Eric Daniels, Peter Homer, Brian Edmunds, Paul Saxon, Christine Thomas, Maureen Jinks, Valerie Russell, Graham Jones. Front row: Valerie Foster, Jean Atkinson, Margaret Ingram, June Gilbert, Edwin Yates. (*Jean Rackham*)

The reception class at Fisher Street School, Christmas 1954. Among the children, from left to right: Michael Causer, Barbara Smith, Michael Crutchley David Fereday, Linda Thompson, Edwin Emms, Maureen Berridge. (*Bertha Griffiths*)

Children from Fisher Street School taking part in a variety concert in the nearby Adult School building, July 1959. Back row, left to right: Christopher Butlin, Sandra Evans, Alan Sharman, Colin Aston. Middle row: Sandra Mills, Margaret Davies, Linda Boughton. Front row: Susan Price David Pitt, Raymond Martin, Trevor Hickinbottom, Susan Sutton. (*Colin Aston*)

Mrs Weaver's class, Fisher Street School, making festive hats and decorations prior to Christmas 1953. Left-side desks: Maureen Bailey. Middle row, left to right: Judith Green, Pat Small, John Fereday, John Whitehouse, Margaret Weston, Peter Homer, Linda Whitehouse, Pat Tillison. Far right: Maureen Morgan, ? Ralph, Arthur Parry. (*Lily Weaver*)

An infants class at Fisher Street School, *c.* 1924. Back row, left to right: Jack Newell, -?-, -?-, Norman Saxon, Harry Basford, John Edmunds, Dennis Saxon. Fourth row: -?-, -?-, Jimmy Sinar, Tom Abass, Bert Jones, George Gardner, Dan Yates, Arthur Parry. Third row: Kathy Hartshorne, Eileen Holden, -?-, Myra Thompson, -?-, -?-, -?-, -?-, Alec Parsons. Second row: -?-, -?-, May Merchant, -?-, ? Beacham, Dorothy Markham, Horace Cresswell. Front row: -?-, -?-, -?-, Edna Parsons, -?-, -?-, -?-, Mary Cutler. (*Arthur Parry*)

Classmates of 1937 pose for a photograph in the school playground at Fisher Street. Back row, left to right: ? Law, Dennis Jones, Billy Green, Colin Boyes, ? Law. Middle row: Elizabeth Reynolds, Irene Reid, -?-, Betty Hancock, Joyce Todd, Dorothy Davies. Front row: -?-, -?-, Billy Bourton. (*Frank Reynolds*)

The annual school photograph at Fisher Street, *c.* 1958. Back row, third from left: Linda Sargent. Among those in the middle section: John Johnson, John Hunt, Philip Shaw, Trevor Smith, Robert Berridge, Ray Hickman, Alan Dunn, Malcolm Beckett, David Hamblett, Michael Causer, Melvyn Abrahams, Keith Knight, David Bingham. Second row, first left: Christine Markham. Front row, first and second left; Joy Reynolds Linda Fereday. (*Christine Henson*)

A very early picture of pupils at Fisher Street School, *c.* 1919. Harry Sowry is on the back row, extreme right, with Horace Bailey next to him. Tommy Tilley (left) and William Riley (right) are at each end of the fourth row. Second row, left to right: second and third: Jessie Jinks, Doris Whitworth. Front row: Annie Whitton, -?-. (*Helen Boyes*)

Parents visit Miss Bertha Griffiths' infants class during an open day at Fisher Street School, *c.* 1948. Among those in the back row, from left to right, are: Assistant Miss Pugh, Bertha Griffiths, Rose Baker and pupil Ken Hunter. Middle section: Joan Price, Ann Holt, Maureen Parry, Alan Bratt, Ann Nightingale, Janet Macdadd. Front row: -?-, -?-, Michael Burns, -?-, Barbara Aston, Ben Powell, -?-. (*Bertha Griffiths*)

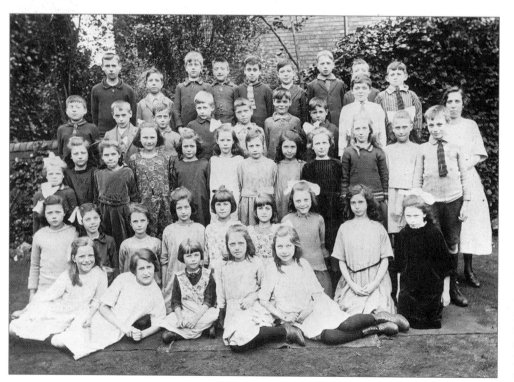

This early picture of a Fisher Street School junior class was taken in the playground, c. 1923. The boy in the back row, fourth from the left is Tommy Toon while on the front row, fourth and fifth from the left are Gladys Ball and Becky Roper. (*Elsie Pritchard*)

The infants nursery class at Fisher Street School, Great Bridge, *c.* 1925. On the left of the picture are: Norman Adams, Tommy Adkins, Miriam Gilson, Clara Bailey. In the centre: Sammy Dunn, Christiana Jackson, Irene Ore. On the right: Nellie Downes, Ron Smith, Bill Hunt, Sam Hollowood, Harry Stott. (*Christiana Townsend*)

Concert party participants pictured in the playground at Fisher Street School, *c.* 1935. Back row, left to right: Stanley Bratt, Denis Bratt, Arthur Reece, Howard Clarke, Gordon Hall, Gordon Thomas, -?-. Middle row: Gwen Fardell, Aileen Mincher, Irene Melia, Amy Fisher, Annie Henshaw, Iris Vanes, Doreen Worley, Dorothy Williams. Front row: Brian Fellows, Roy Parkes, Alan Brookes. (*Iris Gill*)

A Fisher Street School infants class, *c.* 1945. Back row, second from left: John Wood. Fifth row, second from left: Maurice Knight. Third row, left to right: Margaret Jones, -?-, Geoffrey Wyant, -?-, Colin Maul, Sheila Slater, John Bradburn, Billy Wherton. Second row: -?-, -?-, -?-, -?-, -?-, Billy Nock, Derek Abrahams, Rita Martin. Front row: -?-, -?-, John Woodhall, -?-, Danny Stokes, Fred Lawley, Ray Barnfield. (*Ray Barnfield*)

An infants class at Fisher Street School, *c.* 1938. Back row, left to right: George Emms, Doreen Wylde, Doreen Wright, Jean Small, Sheila Banner, Melva Cottrell, Betty Day, Doreen Bird. Middle row: Doreen Harris, Brenda Weston, Brenda Woodhall, Mary Aston, Iris Ward, Violet Jones, Margaret Parkes. Front row: Reg Jarvis, -?-, Margaret Richards, Lilian Ore, -?-, Mary Haycock, Violet Payne. (*Brenda Willetts*)

This studious picture shows a sewing group in the playground of Fisher Street School, *c.* 1937. Back row, left to right: Elizabeth Coley, Pauline Johnson, Joan Day. Front row: Rose Weston, Iris Vanes, Barbara Shepherd. (*Iris Gill*)

Miss Powell's class, Fisher Street School, *c.* 1930. Among the back row, left to right, Mary Hunt, Doreen Anderson. Sixth row: Joan Sayce, Joyce Homer, Alfred Vanes, Sarah Smith, Dorothy Nock. Fifth row: Gwen Clarke, Ted Bunch, Horace Jones. Fourth row: Lily Edmunds, Arthur Martin, Ray Addis, John Webb, Bill Homer, Nora Whitehouse, Maud Howells. Third row: Joan Dodd, John Grainger, Eileen Draper, Gwen Markham. Second row: Florrie Cox, Betty Saunders, Norman Riley, Douglas Brettle, Jacky Webb, Doris Niblett, Violet Clarke, May Fields. Front row: Dorothy Wilkes, Selwyn Howells, Florrie Hickinbottom, May Bradley. (*May Haines*)

Nursery rhymes were the theme for this concert party held in Fisher Street School, *c.* 1958. Back row, left to right: Gordon Richards, Anita Freeman, Barbara Stringer, Lynn Cooper, Susan Markham, Brenda Cope, Linda Thompson, Michael Causer, June Ellis. Middle row: Terry Johnson, Ralph Moore. Front row: Michael Crutchley, Angela Cheadle, Carol Gilbert, Iris Lowe, Terry Hann. (*Monica Richards*)

Deputy Headmaster Frank Wootton stands behind his Fisher Street School football team at Great Bridge, *c.* 1957. Back row, left to right: George Harris, Michael Harman, John Aston, Geoffrey Roper, Paul ?, David Marsden, ? Partridge. Front row: Brian Stott, Ted Sutton, Roderick Hill, Michael Parry, Jimmy Ridgeway. (*Bertha Griffiths*)

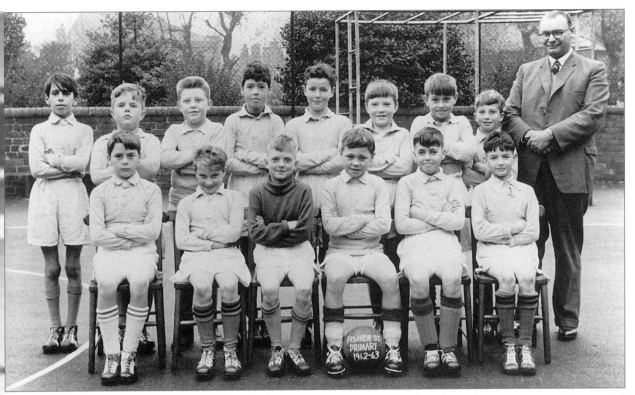

Fisher Street School FC, 1962/3, in the playground with sportsmaster Norman Riley. Back row, left to right: David Worley, Edwin Emms, -?-, Stanley Jones, Colin Aston, -?-, Billy Walls, -?-, Norman Riley. Front row: Malcolm Knight, David Hamblett, Carl Bailey, Peter Roberts, Alan Cartwright, -?-. (*Colin Aston*)

Pictured on Greets Green 'Rec' in 1966 are members of the Fisher Street School football team. Back row, left to right: David Edwards, Norman Riley. Middle row: Paul Cope, Tony Corbett, Nigel Bailey, Robert Parkes, Keith Jones, Graham Cox. Front row: Leslie Foster, Kenneth Hoskins, Michael Smith, Melvyn Hamblett, Glyn Hodgkisson, David Edwards, Jeffrey Green. (*Monica Richards*)

Greets Green School country dance teams, 1946–7. Back row, left to right: Miss Baker, Joan Boswell, Iris Henley, Mavis Brookes, Pat Jones, Betty Ralph, Gwen Nason, Shirley Stanway, Monica Benson, Joyce Griffiths, Margaret Carr, Elsie Merris. Middle row: Joan Edwards, Hilda Smith, Lorna Plevey, Vera Phillips, Janet Pearson, Margaret Lee, Audrey Smith, Joyce Pitt, Queenie Prince, Cathy Bevan, Margaret Martin, Sheila Ruston, G.H. 'Cocky' Woodward. Front row: Betty Tandy, Valerie Cadman, Doreen Abrahams, Alma Smith, Pat Brown, Joan Smith, Jean Barnfield, Joan ?, Betty Lowe, Cynthia Weston. (*Joyce Stimpson*)

'Briar Rosebud' as portrayed by Joan Day in a tableau at Fisher Street School, *c.* 1932. Back row, left to right: Ida Stokes, Nora Meredith, Dorothy Evans, Ethel Riley. Front row: Gwen Emms, -?-, -?-, -?-, Joan Day, Irene Melia, -?-. (*Dorothy Wheatley*)

A smartly dressed group of Greets Green Junior School pupils pose for the annual photo call, *c.* 1929. Back row, left to right: Arthur Rolls, Leslie Dunn, John 'Ginger' Fox, -?-, -?-. Middle row: Stan Franks, William Elwell, Frank Edmunds, -?-, -?-, Eugene Lloyd. Front row: Jimmy Ruston, -?-, -?-, Harry Woodward, ? Shaw. (*Nora Woodward*)

School friends pictured at the front of Greets Green School, Whitehall Road, selling flags commemorating Alexandra Rose Day, *c.* 1933. In the background can be seen Ryders Green Road with Harry Turner's butchers premises on the left corner next to Dora Beach's cake shop. Back row: -?-, -?-. Front row, left to right: Mary Kimberley, Jean Arnold, Joan Tandy. (*Jean Beddow*)

Greets Green School swimming shield winners, *c.* 1928. Back row, left to right: -?-, -?-, John Walker, Walter Turner, George Homer, Jack Holmes, -?-, Arthur Parry, Harold Gibbons, Ted Rudge, Bob Holden, -?-, Jimmy Brookes. Third row: -?-, Jack Newell, Jack Burns, -?-, -?-, -?-, Jack Lane, Sam Francis, -?-, -?-, ? Timmins, Ted Forrester, -?-, Walter Westbury, -?-. Second row: -?-, Jack Rutter, Fred Markham, -?-, -?-, -?-, Bill Calloway, Jack Arnold, -?-, Dan Yates. Front row: -?-, ? Forrester, ? Perkins, -?-. (*Arthur Parry*)

Greets Green School FC, May 1970. Back row, left to right: Steven Cooksey, Philip Collinson, David Aveline, Paul Langley, Terry Purcell, Ian Fisher, Steve Cutler. Front row: Michael Law, Mark Newey, Mark Whitehouse, Wayne Hill, Dean Barnes, David Thomas. (*Evelyn Purcell*)

Greets Green School FC, 1938/9, pictured with sportsmaster T.G. Summerton and headmaster G.H. 'Cocky' Woodward. Back row, left to right: Harry Bird, Edgar Cox, Harold Lester, Harold Smith, Derek Wilkins. Middle row: James Churms, Alan Rushton, T.G. Summerton, G.H. Woodward, Stanley Lloyd, Jack Goodwin. Front row: Arthur Bowen, Horace Robinson. (*Harold Lester*)

Greets Green School FC, season 1950/1. Back row, left to right: Jack Shipley, Thomas G. Summerton, Cyril Williams, Alec Wilson. Middle row: Eddie Jones, Brian Attwell, Brian Stanway, David Moore, Jim Powell, -?-, Ralph Sherwood, Geoff Whitehouse. Front row: Victor Markham, Gordon Weston, Tom Hughes, -?-, Brian Ford, Keith Markham, Len Wilson. (*Gordon Weston*)

An unusual picture showing children eating their lunch at Great Bridge Infants School, Mount Street, *c.* 1947. Many youngsters experienced the delights of school dinners in those halcyon days but not everyone had the occasion photographed. Around the table in the background, second from the left: Raymond Foster, third from the left: Michael Moore. (*Raymond Foster*)

This picture of Great Bridge School Infants Class in Mount Street was taken just a few weeks before the start of the Second World War in 1939. The pupils were blissfully unaware that within two years enemy bombs would be dropping near their classroom and devastating many of the surrounding buildings. Lily Cox is seated in front of the teacher, with Hazel Ashcroft to her left. (*Lily King*)

Great Bridge School, Mount Street, *c.* 1934. Back row, left to right: Evelyn Gould, -?-, Doreen Wood, Ivy Lewis, ? Coley, Dorothy Maund, Eileen Nicklin, Connie Fox, -?-, Violet Jones, -?-, Violet Stevenson. Third row: -?-, -?-, Winnie Hyde, Betty ?, -?-, Peggy Ashcroft, Nellie Homer, Florrie Howes, May Bunce, Nancy Hughes, Nellie Evans, Gwen Bannister, Jean Worsley, Christine Griffiths, -?-. Second row: ? Stevenson, -?-, Florrie Powell, -?-, Joan Lappage, Laura Bellingham, -?-, Agnes ?, Vera Evans, Jessie Hill. Front row: Vera Hughes, -?-, -?-, -?-, -?-, Cissy Roper. (*Doreen Nicholls*)

Mount Street, Great Bridge inter-schools rounders team, *c.* 1980. Back row, left to right: Jayshree Patel, Donna Walker, Anita Harris, Hilary Norton, Penny Pittaway, Mandy Wilson, Gail Tudor. Front row: Alison Burns, Julie Perry, Beverley Moore, Samantha Thomas, Maureen Greenfield, Terry Keasey (Headmaster). (*Jean Williams*)

Santa Claus visits an infants class at Great Bridge School, Mount Street during Christmastide 1912. The headmaster at the time was Charles Greenwood, the headmistress Louisa Hickinbottom and infants mistress Elizabeth Walker. The school was built in 1873 to accommodate 400 boys and 257 girls and was enlarged in 1887 to cater for a further 256 infants. (*Arthur Stacey*)

A gathering of pupils and staff at Great Bridge School, Mount Street, on the occasion of caretaker Len Whitehouse's retirement, *c.* 1974. Back row, left to right: Margaret Clews, Jean Douglas, Molly Boughton, Sheila Aston, Lily Roberts, Maud Whitehouse, Sandy Bradie, Len Whitehouse, Ken Bates, Monica Richards, Peggy Patrick, Beryl Nash. Among the children on the right of the picture are: Clive Roberts, Susan Hunt, Amanda Fullwood. (*Monica Richards*)

A Christmas party at Great Bridge School, Mount Street, *c.* 1952. The headmistress was Miss Millicent Kendrick. Back row, left to right; -?-, Barbara ?, -?-, -?-, -?-, -?-. Third row: Margaret Chance, Kathleeen Doody, Maureen Poulton, Margaret Davis, Joyce Round. Second row: Ann Doleman, Mary Blakesley, Valerie Lines, Eileen Street, Zena Tothill. Front row: Joan King, -?-, -?-, Linda Hall. (*Linda Jones*)

Staff at Great Bridge Infants School, Mount Street, line up for a photograph in the assembly hall, *c.* 1970. Back row, left to right: Brenda Walker, Beryl Nash, Goubach Uhbi, Margaret Clews, Lillian Copper, Edith Mathers, Joyce Knight. Front row: Molly Boughton, Bertha Griffiths, Sheila Aston (Headmistress), Ivy Wainwright, Rose Bache. (*Brenda Walker*)

Winners of the John Toy Banner in an inter-schools play competition held in Birmingham, *c.* 1930, were pupils of St Peter's Council School, Great Bridge, pictured here on the vicarage lawn. Left to right: Irene Dunn, Mary Calloway, Eva Reeves, Joan Morris (kneeling), Florrie Davies, Mary Stockel (seated), Jim Dugmore, Muriel Bevan (kneeling), Nancy Slater, Gladys Baker, Mary Paskin. (*Mary Rose*)

Pupils of St Peter's Council School, Whitehall Road, *c.* 1928, showing in the background an access gate to the church. Back row, third from the left: Edith Curtis. Middle row: Mary Allway, -?-, Lily Tolly, Mary Toon, Mary Bratt, -?-, Frances Haywood. Front row, -?-, Joan Thompson, Edna Hill, Violet Richards, -?-. (*David Allway*)

Chapter Six
Work, Leisure & People

Signalman Fred Shirley inside Great Bridge North signal-box on the South Staffordshire railway line, *c.* 1961. Born at 44 Fisher Street, Great Bridge, on 7 April 1919, Fred joined British Railways on 6 November 1946 after serving seven years in the Suffolk Regiment during the Second World War, three of which were spent as a Japanese Prisoner of War in the infamous Changi Gaol, Singapore. After twenty years on the railways and another sixteen with the CEGB and MEB, Fred eventually retired in April 1984. (*Nigel Hazelwood*)

Screen & Screen, engineers and millwrights, Limerick Engine Works, Meeting Street, Great Bridge, *c*. 1910. The firm was established in 1902 by Ernest and Thomas Screen (centre), whose other business interests were the supply of lorries and cars. This diversification, however, could not prevent eventual closure taking place in 1934. (*T.J.H. Price*)

Floor moulder Brian Ruston venting the core for a cast-iron pot prior to baking in the foundry of James W. Shenton Ltd, Tinsley Street, Great Bridge. Observing are the Mayor and Mayoress of West Bromwich, Councillor Joseph Hubbard and his wife Katherine, who in 1965 were visiting the firm to open new office premises. The business was founded in Mill Street, Great Bridge, in 1905 by James and James William Shenton, who by 1912 had moved the foundry to its present Tinsley Street site. From left to right; Albert Serrel, Ken Shenton, Ruby Shenton, Katherine Hubbard, Joseph Hubbard, Alan Shenton, Brian Ruston. (*Brian Ruston*)

The polishing shop of Kingfisher Ltd, Charles Street, Great Bridge, *c.* 1952. The firm was established around 1850 by William Fisher, a builder of 238 High Street, West Bromwich who by 1880 had also become a school desk manufacturer. Between 1884 and 1906 he was operating exclusively in the latter capacity from 53 Paradise Street before moving in 1907 to Charles Street, where the company became known as 'Kingfisher'. Back row, left to right: Bill Overfield, Brenda Tinsley. Middle row: Jean Sheldon, Ann Bunch, Eadie Webb, Emily Amos, Elsie ?, Sylvia Brown, Nell Cope. Front row: Florrie Timmins, Ada Burton, Harriet Pitt. (*Colin Boyes*)

A steam traction engine pauses in West Bromwich High Street, *c.* 1925, during the transportation of this magnificent boiler made by William Chattaway Ltd, constructional engineers, Mill Street, Great Bridge. Curiously, however, the company undertaking the movement are rival boilermakers Harper & Screen of Brades Hall, Oldbury. (*Alan Price*)

Edward Lissimore, cart and coach builder, Brickhouse Lane, Great Bridge, *c*. 1910. The business, which was established near the post office in 1901, was originally a shoeing forge contracted to the L&NW Railway Co. In 1926, six years after moving into motor body building and repairs, the firm changed its name to the Central Shoeing Forge. (*T.J.H. Price*)

Employees of the Warwick Rim & Sectioning Co. Ltd, Bagnall Street, Golds Hill, pose for a photograph during their works outing to Blackpool, *c*. 1936. The young boy pictured left with the toy boat, Jack Hughes, was later to become a professional with Walsall FC. Back row, left to right: Jack Hughes, Elizabeth Hughes, -?-, -?-, Norman Rutter, Arthur Foster, Herbert Hughes, -?-, Billy Grant. Front: Norman Walters, Alan Hughes, -?-. (*Janet Hughes*)

Degreasing, phosphating and varnishing tubulars and fittings in preparation for the assembly line at the Wellington Tube Works, Brickhouse Lane, Great Bridge, *c.* 1963. The firm's name may have referred to the 'Iron Duke' (1769–1852) but curiously, like the nearby pub and coach works, the title Wellington was not adopted until many years after his death. Pictured in fitting shop No. 23 where Ray Dicken was foreman are, from left to right: Olive Wilkes, Margaret ?, -?-, Alice Weston. (*Geoff Paddock/Hughes & Holmes Ltd*)

Carpenters on a tea break in the workshop of the Great Bridge Cabinet Co. Ltd in Mill Street pictured just two years before closure in 1981. Managing Director Reg Worthington had previously carried on the business from the rear of 69 Great Bridge, near greengrocer A.H. Adams & Sons. From left to right: Ron Simkins, John ?, Brian Jones, Sid Bayliss, -?-, Mike Boyes, Noel Hadley. (*Colin Boyes*)

Workers pictured at the firm of P.H. Muntz & Barwell, Alexandra Works, Great Bridge Street, *c.* 1955. Philip Henry Muntz established the firm here in 1864 taking over premises which had previously been owned by a timber merchant. Prior to closure in April 1991 Muntz & Barwell had been a major manufacturer and exporter of brass and copper tubes. Back row, left to right: -?-, -?-, Joe Franks. Front row: Jim Whitehouse, Philip Franks, Harry Day. (*Katherine McMahon-Stone*)

Steel Parts Ltd, Brickhouse Lane, Great Bridge, executive and staff dinner held in the Prince's Suite at the New Inns Hotel Handsworth on 18 April 1952. Heading the entertainment bill was radio star Eric Barker while music was provided by Basil Henderson and his band. Foreground: -?-, George Sherwood, Winnie Overton. Second table, left to right: Stan Wilkins, Joan Wilkins, -?-, -?-, -?-, Albert Skidmore, Horace ?, Mrs Skidmore. (*Stan Wilkins*)

Girder yard employees of Horseley Bridge & Thomas Piggott Ltd, Horseley Road, Great Bridge, *c.* 1936. Back row, left to right: Charlie Millard, Charlie Steventon, Frank Walker, Bill Wheale, Arthur Appleby, Albert Morgan, Bert Stanley, ? Easthope. Third row: George Stimpson, Reg Stanton, Charlie Hemmings, George Young, George Perkins. Second row: Wilf Green, Walter Hartland, Frank Harris, Jack Shuker, William Lilley, Nemia Clarke, Len Bullas, Eric Kitson Bill Griffin, Joe Chattaway. Front row: Ernie Cope, ? Cope, Ernie Barham, -?-, ? Packwood, ? Barham, ? Easthope, Bill Ashmore. (*Bill Wheale*)

Employees of the Wellington Tube Works, Brickhouse Lane, Great Bridge, photographed after receiving awards for twenty-five years' service, *c.* 1959. Back row, left to right: Sammy Merchant, Leonard Markham, Elisha Richards, George Upton, Jack Green, -?-, Albert Markham, -?-. Front row: Jack Pincher, -?-, Edward Cottrell, -?-, Roger Turner, Ernie Cox, Jack Dean, Cyril Dawes. (*Brenda Stokes*)

Employees of Kingfisher Ltd, Charles Street, Great Bridge, on a River Thames boat trip to Windsor Castle during the Festival of Britain celebrations of 1951. The upper deck includes: Ray Whitehouse, Fred Parton, Margaret Parton, Joan Canning, Ray Canning, Alan Trend, Ted Welsh, Harry Pottinger, Sylvia Brown, Ann Eggington, John Anchorite, Sylvia Johnson, Iris Smith, John Webb, Arthur Evans, Brian James. (*Ray Canning*)

Fitters and electricians at Robinson Brothers Ltd, chemical manufacturers, Ryders Green, *c.* 1967. Back row, left to right: Arthur Cooper, Bob Carter, John Cooke, George Woodfield, Ron Marshall, Ken Jones. Third row: Mick Hodgetts, Vic Hendon, Keith Simms. Second row: Alan Cadman, Fred MacDonald, Sam Cole, Tony Whitehouse, Gordon Rooke, Sam Pincher, Albert Langford, Peter Sharman. Front row: Jack Worley, Fred Smith, Terry Howes, Victor Bagnall, Albert Hinton, Ken Ford. (*Ken Ford*)

Long-service and retired employees of Kingfisher Ltd, Charles Street, Great Bridge attending a Christmas lunch at the headquarters of their parent company, Educational Supplies Association Ltd, in Stevenage, Herts, *c.* 1960. Back row, second from the left: Jack Sheldon. Middle row: -?-, Herbert Reason, Cyril Tack, George Aston, Bill Aston, Jack Poulton, Vera Corfield, -?-, -?-, Albert Bunch, Frank Bullock, Les Pearce, Harry Massey. Front row: George Mason, Reg Tolliday, -?-, W.H. Phipps, Florrie Stevens, Arthur Holden. (*David Malborn*)

Children's Christmas party (hosted by Braithwaites & Co. Ltd, Henry Street, Great Bridge) held for employees' children in the works canteen, *c.* 1952. Among the parents standing on the back row, third from left: Emily Harris. Third from right: Sally Howes. Front row, left to right: -?-, -?-, -?-, -?-, Keith Markham, Victor Markham, Derek Harris, Roy Harris, Tony Harris (behind Roy), Leslie Harris. (*Sally Howes*)

Staff attending Ratcliffs (GB) Ltd annual dinner held in a top London hotel, *c.* 1960. From left to right (clockwise): Eric Bedwin, Josie Phipps, Harry Jeans, Norma Wickett, Betty Bluck, Lawson Garbett, Nancy Hill, Geoff Pickering, Doreen Roberts. (*Geoff Pickering*)

The annual outing to Worcester of Samuel Pearson's glassworks, Charles Street, Great Bridge, *c.* 1949. This famous firm of glass-blowers, established in 1888, was a major manufacturer of bottles and jars before closure in 1970. The group includes: Bert Cresswell, Harry Ralph, Harry Arter, Bill Bowen, Joe Saunders, Jim Rose, Tommy Cox, Jack Shaw, Cyril Albrighton, Peggy Albrighton Sandra Albrighton, Mary Rose, Harry Day, Harold Whitehouse, Harry Bishop, Freddy Smith, May Smith, Doris Abbotts, Jack Franks, Ester Greenfield, Anne Pearce, Derek Pearce, Billy Pearce, Gary Albrighton, Billy Smith, Ray Abbotts, Bill Leddington, Harry Rose. (*Jim Rose*)

Medium foundry employees of Rudge Littley Ltd, ironfounders, Phoenix Street, Swan Village, *c.* 1930. The firm, closed in 2001, was originally established in Birmingham before relocating here in 1914. Back row, sixth from the left: Herbert Hunt, eleventh: Jimmy Jackson, twelfth: Harry Green, thirteenth: Bill Bowen, fifteenth: Clarence Corbett. Third row, first and third: Harry Freeman, Jimmy Wylde. Second row, fourth, fifth, sixth: Tom Mayo, Isaac Padmore, Arthur Capewell. Group of three, left: Cyril Hartshorne, -?-, Tom Lappage. Front row, second and fifth: Arthur Edmunds, Joe Coley. (*William Hunt*)

A Christmas party (hosted by Great Bridge Foundry Ltd, Sheepwash Lane) held at Grant Hall, West Bromwich, *c.* 1951, for employees' children. Among those pictured here are Christine Adams, John Adams, Rose Price, Pat Price, Valerie Price, Paul Cox, Ron Harrison. (*Sam Price*)

Volunteer members of the Wellington Tube Works' St Johns Ambulance Brigade pictured on the firm's bowling green in Brickhouse Lane, *c.* 1939. Back row, left to right: ? Richards, -?-, William Parker, Walter Sims, -?-, -?-, Tom Corbett, Cyril Haden. Middle row: Arthur 'Curley' Maddox, Arthur Dawes, Jimmy Dickins, -?-, Tom Austin, ? Smith, -?-, Herbert Powell. Front row: ? Coley, Jack Dean, Bill Randle, Tom Dean, Norman Johnson, Albert Randle, Ben Simcox. (*Walter Sims*)

Wellington Tube Works', Brickhouse Lane, Great Bridge, annual camping holiday to Abergele, 1939. Back row, fourth from the left: Leonard Markham. Seventh row, first left: Walter Sims. Sixth row, second left (vertical striped shirt): Daniel Sims. Others include: Sammy Merchant, Frank Wilkes, Joe Smith, Vic Bevan, Elisha Richards, Jimmy Arter, Stan Markham, Douglas Turner, Alfred Fullwood, Billy Fellows, Cyril Page, Jimmy Icke, Cliff Talbot, Billy Beckett, Tommy Burns. (*Brenda Stokes*)

The late Duke of Kent being presented to long-service employees of Horseley Bridge & Thomas Piggott Ltd. outside their first aid surgery, 14 April 1942. From left to right: Sam Ellis, -?-, Jack Gage, Bill Smith, Bill Archer, Frank Davies, Bill Baillie (back to camera), Bert Hinley, -?-, Duke of Kent, Lord Dudley, Arthur Dyson, -?-, -?-, Leon Harper, -?-. (*Beryl Martin*)

Tipton Red Cross volunteer nurses pictured at the rear of Horseley Road clinic, Great Bridge, *c*. 1943. Back row, left to right: Betty Whitehouse, Olive Love, Doreen Brown, Molly Clay, Brenda Shipley, Evelyn Handley. Third row: Lorna Mills, Jean Strathearn, Joan Fisher, Josie Standford, Hilary Jenkins, -?-, Gertie Paskin. Second row: Lottie Gwynne, Eileen Bowater, Nellie Whitehouse, Jessie Gould, Jean Whitehouse, Joan Bratt, -?-. Front row: -?-, Joan Bailey, ? King, ? Bowen, Margaret Smith, Gwen Brookes, -?-. (*Doreen Shelley*)

A Stanier Class '8F' goods locomotive No. 48335 on the Bescot to Round Oak run, via Dudley, takes on water alongside the 'up' platform on Great Bridge North railway station, *c.* 1961. On the right a 'Bank' engine of a similar class, No. 48734, is waiting to assist during the climb to Dudley (*Nigel Hazlewood*)

The *J.T. Daly* 0–4–0 saddle tank steam locomotive used for shunting flat wagons within the confines of Horseley Piggott Engineering Works, Great Bridge. Pictured with their engine outside the maintenance department, *c.* 1961, are driver George Rushton and, bottom right, shunter Jimmy Rostance. The locomotive was purchased in 1931 from W.G. Bagnall Ltd of Stafford for the sum of £1,200 and named after Horseley's Chairman James T. Daly. It now operates as a tourist attraction in Jersey. (*Nigel Hazlewood*)

Management and staff of Brickhouse Foundry Ltd, Brickhouse Lane, 1974, manufacturers of manhole covers and in former years producers of cast iron bridges and weighbridge plates. The company was established in 1858 but little is known about their early history other than the proprietors were predominantly members of the Kendrick family. After the death of one F.W. Turton in 1944, the business was registered as a Limited Company by its new owner, Ralph Godfrey, a man considered by his employees to be a gentleman. Between 1944 and 1948 a major renovation programme was completed which greatly improved working conditions and the company's image. Brickhouse Foundry became a public company in 1967 and following a merger with competitors Dudley & Dowell, Cradley Heath the same year, they changed their name to the Brickhouse Dudley Group. Nineteen years later in 1986 the firm became part of Glynwed International who, having closed the Cradley foundry in 1992, sold the rest of the Brickhouse Group to the French company Saint Gobain in 1997. Then on 29 October 1999 Brickhouse Foundry in Great Bridge was also closed down. Left to right: Nancy Halford, Dorothy Kaye, Joan James, Ivy Round-Hancock, Horace Carter, Bill Bolton, Sue Williams, Barbara Severn, Sue Bowen, Ann Lake, Bob Wright, Keith Cherrington, Keith Jones, Alf Douglas. (*Keith Cherrington*)

Children and parents gather on the 'down' platform of Great Bridge North railway station, *c.* 1925, in preparation for an excursion to the seaside. The trip was probably organised by one or more of the many day and Sunday schools in the area, although a number of local firms also made similar arrangements for their employees' children. Among the crowd is Fisher Street resident Charles Shaw who was the station master here from 1917 to 1929. In the background, beyond the booking office and waiting rooms, are the Eagle Road premises of iron and steel manufacturers Roberts & Cooper Ltd (extreme right) with coal merchant William Charles occupying the small building left of centre which was previously owned by Swan Tavern licensee Solomon Gould. This railway station, which dealt mainly with goods traffic, was on the L&NWR South Staffordshire line and when it opened on 1 May 1850 it had the distinction of being the first in Tipton. The drastic overhaul of the rail network during the 'Beeching era' of the 1960s sounded the death-knell for small stations such as these, and as a consequence Great Bridge North was closed to passengers on 4 May 1964 and to goods in December 1967. (*Lilian Shaw*)

Literally a flying visit to the Isle of Man organised by Ratcliffs (GB) Ltd for their employees, *c.* 1951. On the stairway: Freddy Barton, Cecil Palmer, Olive Holtom, ? Pritchard, Nancy Hill, Betty Bluck. Front row, left to right: Frank Bent, -?-, William Murphy, -?-, -?-, Len Martin, George Lawton, Cyril Parkes, -?-, Bob Morgan, -?-, Walter Turner, -?-, -?-, -?-, Albert Sadler, Bill Paskin, Tommy Lloyd, Horace Smith, Edward Ratcliff, Arthur Phillips, -?-. (*Betty Johnson*)

Ratcliffs (GB) Ltd hired West Bromwich Town Hall to hold a party and film show for their employees' children, *c.* 1956. In the front row, left to right: Doris Crutchley, Sam Brown, Michael Crutchley, -?-, -?-, David Nightingale, Philip Nightingale, Irene Nightingale. (*David Nightingale*)

Miss Conex-Sanbra finalists pictured in the works canteen/social club in Whitehall Road, Great Bridge, on 30 April 1971, the eventual winner being number 13, Miss Jean Palmer. Entertainment for this annual event was provided by 'The Concordes'. From left to right: Dorothy Bell, Angela Brookes, Denise Cannel, Susanne Homer, Jean Palmer (winner), Vivienne Skett, -?-, Gerald Fisher, -?-. (Alan Price)

'Our gang' from Brickhouse Lane, Elwell Street and Great Bridge Street get together for a reunion on 29 August 1975 at the Kingfisher Country Club, Wall Heath. Back row, left to right: John Crutchley, John Fereday, Raymond Jinks, Michael Burns, Terry Price, John Palmer, Trevor Jinks, Keith Stubbs. Front row: George Bullock, David Fereday, Brian Edmunds, Brian Shenstone, John Martin, Michael Pace. (T.J.H. Price)

A distinguished gathering at West Bromwich Town Hall for the 1952 annual presentation of allotment trophies. George Ward is pictured receiving the Borough Cup and Shield having won first prize for his allotment in Sheepwash Lane, Great Bridge. Also present are the Mayor and Mayoress of West Bromwich, Councillor Harry Sower and his wife Mary. On the extreme right is the West Bromwich Carnival Queen Kathy Pallfreeman. (*Iris Rich*)

The presentation of a cut glass basket to Ellen Edmunds at Walsall Conduits Ltd, Dial Lane, on her retirement in April 1976, having completed twenty-five years' service from 1930 to 1945 and 1966 to 1976. Back row, left to right: Derek Hickman, Billy Berry, Bess Mercer, Jean Greenhill, Peggy Delicott, Evelyn Turner, Freda Reed, Lily Phillips, Sue Holden. Front row: Peter Graves (Personnel Manager), Ellen Edmunds, Eric Dixon, Frank Best. (*Lily Phillips*)

A 'men only' charabanc outing from the sawmills of Thomas Cox & Sons Ltd, Market Place, Great Bridge, in their timber yard before departure, *c.* 1930. The firm closed around 1970, having being established here in 1828. John Richardson can be seen standing in the centre of the group while foreman Richard Brevitt (white coat) is seated below. (*Annie Ball*)

An outing from the Frogs Meadow Works of Ratcliff & Ratcliff, Golds Hill, *c.* 1929. By 1982 the firm's brass and copper rolling mills were providing employment for over 600 people, but closure came during Christmas 1989, just nine months after the company had been taken over in a £12.5 million deal with Severn plc. Those in the coach include Ernie Stanley, Bert Stanley and Charlie Hogan. (*Cynthia Stokes*)

With Albion gasworks in the background, a rebuilt Patriot class 4–6–0 No. 45535 *Sir Herbert Walker KCB* locomotive and passenger train approaches Albion railway station heading north towards Manchester via Dudley Port on 9 September 1961. The waterway over which the train is passing was the last section of the Thomas Telford New Main Line Canal to be completed, opening in 1838. (*David Williams*)

The Glasgow–Birmingham train hauled by a British Railways Britannia 4–6–2 locomotive No. 70032 *Tennyson* thunders through Albion station and across the level crossing in Union Road, Greets Green. The photograph was taken on 9 September 1961 from the northbound platform looking towards Oldbury. (*David Williams*)

A *c.* 1911 Bowen-Cooke 0–8–0 locomotive No. 49430 on pick-up freight approaches Albion signal-box and railway station heading south towards Birmingham on the Stour Valley line, 1 December 1962. The station, which was located in Union Road, opened in 1853 to serve the growing industrial and residential areas of Albion and Greets Green. Passenger services were withdrawn in 1960 and freight operations had ceased by 1964. (*David Wilson*)

Albion Railway Station viewed from the northbound 'down' platform showing a Birmingham-bound passenger train, hauled by a Stanier 'Black Five' 4–6–0 locomotive No. 45027, passing through on 25 April 1961. Almost obscured, to the right are the station's booking office and waiting room just behind the footbridge steps. (*David Williams*)

Toll End residents and children enjoying themselves at a party in Farm Road celebrating VE Day on 8 May 1945. This happy throng includes: May Evans, Olive Howell, Jean Madeley, Nellie Harrison, Edwin Boughton, ? Nicklin, ? Danks, Mary Smitherman, Jean Buckley, Sheila Crockett, Mabel Edwards, Mary Breeden, Molly Harrison, Charlie Hodgkins, Gwen Bradshaw, Ellen Madeley, Dorothy Price. (*Molly Boughton*)

A VE party on 8 May 1945 for children living in and around Canal Side at the rear of 55–61 Great Bridge where the indoor market now stands. Around the table, from left to right: Beryl Holt, Jean Holt, Ann Holt, Geoff Merchant. Far right: Alf Rayers. Back row, standing: Leah Holt, Nance Merchant, Ethel Nock, -?-, ? Nock, Jim Merchant, ? Smith, Joe Holt. (*Brian Rayers*)

Children in Elwell Street, Great Bridge, awaiting the fancy dress competition results during Queen Elizabeth II coronation day celebrations, 2 June 1953. Back row, left to right: -?-, Sheila Hill, Linda Markham, Gloria Sansome, Ann Stampe, Margaret Markham, -?-, Jennifer Evans. Front row: Michael Kennett (back to camera), Brian Edmunds, John Burns, Trevor Jinks, -?-, -?-, Keith Stubbs, -?-, Margaret Ingram. (*Jennifer Evans*)

Poultney Street residents, Harvills Hawthorn, celebrating at a VE party on 8 May 1945 attended by the Mayor of West Bromwich, Councillor John J. Grant (seated right). Also in the photograph are Edna Andrews, Marion Allsopp, Doreen Ashmore, Marina Roden, Margaret Allsopp, Mr and Mrs Oliver, Gladys Williams, Joyce Williams, Doris Williams, Marge Williams, Joe Williams, Mrs Bennett, Winnie Smith. (*Sue Jackson*)

Parents and children from Elizabeth Road, Greets Green pictured in front of St Peter's School, Whitehall Road following their Queen Elizabeth II coronation day party, 2 June 1953. Among the group are Gordon Abrahams, Gerald Abrahams, Melvin Abrahams, Terry Scotland, Ann Holt, Jean Holt, Pat Shellard, Mrs Shellard, Tony Worley, Fred Worley, Pauline Pitt, Mrs Pitt, Pat Vale, Mrs Vale, Selwyn Vale, Anita Vale, Mrs Perry, Anna Brookes. (*Ann Sheppard*)

Young children taking part in a race along Philip Road, Great Bridge, during celebrations on 2 June 1953 to mark the coronation of Queen Elizabeth II. Race participants include: Susan Tolley (front left), Philip Shaw (front right), and Maurice Hirons. In the crowd of onlookers: Linda Cottrill, Fred Shaw, Mary Jacks, Flossie Fellows, Mabel Price, Alice Cottrill. (*Sam Price*)

Children from the Great Bridge area celebrating the coronation of Queen Elizabeth II at Fisher Street schools, 2 June 1953. Left side of the table, from left to right: -?-, -?-, Trevor Allen, Geoffrey Allen, Michael Aston, Derek Holden, Ray Foster, George Roper. Holding a cup, far end: Freddy Middleton. Right side, fourth from the bottom; John Randle. (*Geoff Allen*)

The Wright family taking time out from their Queen Elizabeth II coronation day festivities to pose for a photograph in the front garden of 46 Stour Street, Greets Green, 2 June 1953. Back row, left to right: Brian Wright, Liz Kane, Ann Wright, Liz Wright, Ray Wright (behind Liz), Isiah (Ike) Wright. Front row: Linda Kane, Dennis Wright, Alan Wright, Walter Wright, Gillian Westwood, Norma Wright, Nita Wright. (*Dot Davies*)

Elwell Street, Great Bridge, *c.* 1930. Locals pose for a photograph on a wall adjoining John and Fanny Belcher's grocery shop on the left (later Sansome's). In the background is a cottage occupied by John and Sarah Holmes which in later years would become the home of Jack and Liza Burns. Back row, left to right: Colin Boyes (baby), Jack Boyes, -?-, Harry Riley, -?-, -?-, Jim ?. Front row: Ernie Markham, -?-. (*Colin Boyes*)

The 9th Tipton (Great Bridge) Girl Guide Company at West Bromwich Town Hall in January 1967. The Mayor, Councillor Joshua Churchman, is demonstrating an 'ultra-modern tape-riter' system which enabled officers all over the town hall to dictate letters to a central typing pool. Also present is the Mayoress, Mrs Violet Churchman, and Guide Captain Dorothy Dando who formed the Company in 1966. (*Joshua Churchman*)

Alderman John Bell JP, elected Mayor of West Bromwich during the municipal years of 1921–2 and 1922–3 was born in 1870 at 220 Great Bridge Street and attended Fisher Street School until the age of thirteen. His forebears were predominantly quarrymen in Scotland and it was from there that Henry Bell, John's great grandfather, came to Great Bridge to work as a mason. John's father, also named Henry, who had married Mary Fletcher in 1850, drove a steam hammer at the forge of Robert Williams & Co.'s ironworks in Brickhouse Lane. When he had to relinquish that occupation in 1854 he built a house in Great Bridge Street where he carried on the business of baker and grocer. His son John, one of eleven children, eventually took over the business around 1894, two years before marrying his first wife, Annie E. Westwood, in 1896. In 1911 he was elected as a Liberal to the West Bromwich Council, representing the Greets Green Ward, a position he held until 1926 when he became an Alderman. Following his second marriage to Dorothy Mary Board in 1925 he continued to play a prominent part in the public and religious life of the area until his retirement in 1958. He died at his Kinver home in 1963. (*Margaret Jeens*)

Councillor Jean Marson JP, who in 2000 became only the second Lady Mayor of the Metropolitan Borough of Sandwell. Born in March 1931 at 100 New Road, Great Bridge, she attended Mount Street and Princes End (joint school) before completing her education at Park Lane Secondary School at the age of fourteen. After joining the labour party in 1978 she first won a seat on Sandwell Council in 1983 representing the Great Bridge ward. Jean has served on numerous committees, including those dealing with leisure services and as Lady Chairman of the legislative body dealing with community care in which she has a particular interest. In 1985 she had the honour of being appointed by the Lord Chancellor to serve as a Justice of the Peace on the West Bromwich Bench. During the municipal year of 1993–4 Jean was made Deputy Mayor to Gwendoline Ivy Wyton JP, the first Lady Mayor of Sandwell. In 2003, Jean will reach another milestone in her political career when she will have represented the people of Great Bridge continuously for a total of twenty years. (*Phil Hill*)

ACKNOWLEGEMENTS

I would like to thank the many friends who loaned me photographs and without whose help this publication would not have been possible. All contributors have been individually acknowledged at the end of each caption. My gratitude is also extended to the following people for providing assistance and additional information:

Doris Abbotts, Annie Ball, Ian Bott, Molly Boughton, John Brimble, Horace Burgess, Jean and Alan Carter, Keith Cherrington, Violet and Joshua Churchman, Norman Cooksey, Dot Davies, Janice Endean, Jackie Evans, Iris Gill, Bertha Griffiths, Nigel Hazelwood, Keith Hodgkins, Ken Hodgkisson, Joan Howes, Wilf Jones, Marie and Walter Kendall, Tony Matthews, Vera Morris, Albert Murphy, Geoffrey Paddock, Cliff Parker, Robin Pearson, Mary Powell, Alan Price, Graham Quinn, Iris Rich, Mary and Jim Rose, Ivy Round-Hancock, Doreen and Maurice Shelly, Trevor Smith, Barry Stokes, Betty and Ron Tedstone, Margaret Tromans, Jean Weston, Sheila Whitehouse, Ned Williams, David Wilson.

I am also grateful to: Asda Supermarket – Tipton, *Birmingham Post & Mail*, Eardley Lewis, Sandwell Libraries, James W. Shenton Ltd, Walsall Local History Centre, *Wolverhampton Express & Star*.

Many thanks also to Ann Castle and all the staff at Asda Supermarket, Great Bridge.

Thanks also to Dr Carl Chinn MBE for his support and encouragement.

Finally, my special thanks once again to *Kathleen Homeshaw* for typing the manuscript.

THE BLACK COUNTRY SOCIETY

This voluntary society, affiliated to the Civic Trust, was founded in 1967 as a reaction to the trend of the late 1950s and early 1960s to amalgamate everything into large units and in the Midlands to sweep away the area's industrial heritage in the process.

The general aim of the Society is to create interest in the past, present and future of the Black Country, and early on it campaigned for the establishment of an industrial museum. In 1975 the Black Country Living Museum was started by Dudley Borough Council on 26 acres of totally derelict land adjoining the grounds of Dudley Castle. This has developed into an award-winning museum which attracts over 250,000 visitors annually.

In 1998 the Museum Board secured a lottery grant of nearly £3 million towards the £4.5 million cost of building a state-of-the-art interpretation centre. Known as the Rolfe Street Baths Project as it incorporated that Smethwick building which was transferred to the museum site, it was officially opened on 18 May 2001. It includes two fine exhibition halls, administration and storage rooms and retains the original Victorian building's façade. The museum's already wide range of attractions is likely soon to be increased in the field of transport with the acquisition of two major collections of vehicles.

At the Black Country Living Museum there is a boat dock fully equipped to restore narrowboats of wood and iron and different vessels can be seen on the dock throughout the year. From behind the Bottle and Glass Inn visitors can travel on a canal boat into Dudley Canal Tunnel, a memorable journey to see spectacular limestone caverns and the fascinating Castle Mill Basin.

There are 2,650 members of the Black Country Society and all receive the quarterly magazine *The Blackcountryman*, of which 136 issues have been published since its founding in 1967. In the whole collection there are some 2,000 authoritative articles on all aspects of the Black Country by historians, teachers, researchers, students, subject experts and ordinary folk with an extraordinary story to tell. The whole constitutes a unique resource about the area and is a mine of information for students and researchers who frequently refer to it. Many schools and libraries are subscribers. Over 3,300 copies of the magazine are printed each quarter. It is non-commercial, and contributors do not receive payment for their articles.

PO Box 71 · Kingswinford · West Midlands DY6 9YN